For my wonderful, worldwide
knitting and crochet community.

Editor: Shawna Mullen
Designer: onethread design, inc.
Production Manager: Kathleen Gaffney

Principal Photography: Traci Goudie
Styling: Vickie Howell
Tech Editor: Chaitanya Muralidhara
Schematics: Tristan Howell
Makeup: Jessi Pagel

Library of Congress Control Number: 2018958268

ISBN: 978-1-4197-3279-9
eISBN: 978-1-68335-668-4

ABRAMS The Art of Books
195 Broadway, New York, NY 10007
abramsbooks.com

the knit vibe

A Knitter's Guide to Creativity,
Community, and Well-being
for Mind, Body, & Soul

by vickie howell

Creator of *The Knit Show*

PRINCIPAL PHOTOGRAPHY BY TRACI GOUDIE

con

6   **Introduction**

PART ONE: THE MAKER

10   **The Profiles**
       Bristol Ivy
15   Kaffe Fassett
20   London Kaye
24   Trisha Malcolm,
       Vogue Knitting
28   Caitlin Hunter,
       Boyland Knitworks
31   Candice English,
       The Farmer's Daughter Fibers
34   Nicky Epstein
37   Julia Madill,
       Yarnspirations
40   Brittany, B.hooked
44   Erika Knight

48   **The Community**
50   Amy Small,
       Knit Collage Indian Co-op
53   Jayna Zweiman,
       The Welcome Blanket Project
56   Krista Suh,
       The Pussyhat Project
60   Brini Maxwell &
       Josh Bennett
63   Diva Zappa,
       The Emilio Scarf Project

Contents

66 Siedah Garrett
70 Elisabeth Ward, Hand.Made.
73 The Knit Hive

74 **The Intention**
Knitting & the Body
76 Yoga for Knitters, Alicia Montoya
79 Exercises for Core Strength & Stability, Britny Fowler
82 Dietary Recommendations for Healthy Bones, Joints, & Muscles, Dr. Michelle Lane

Knitting & the Mind
84 The Neuroscience of Creativity & Mindfulness and Knitting, Chelsea DeKryuff, MA, LPC

Knitting & Spirituality
86 Spinning, Knitting & Judaism, Rabbi Susan Elkodsi
92 Knitting & the Catholic Ritual of Eucharistic Adoration
94 Native American Dye Stuff Harvesting Ritual, Candice English
96 Yarn Craft & Paganism, Christiane Knight

100 Knitter's Astrology, Kerriann Godwin
104 Knitting & Numerology, Dr. Felicia Bender

PART TWO: THE MAKING

The Unexpected
110
112 Mega Crochet Rug, Vickie Howell
114 Hoop Art, Andrea Brinkley
116 Mondo Cable Wall Hanging, Vickie Howell
118 Bold Baskets, Vickie Howell

120 **Go-To Gifts**
122 Go-To Gradient Scarf
124 Go-To Cabled Mittens
126 Go-To Market Bag
130 Go-To Slouchy Beanie
133 Go-To Wrist Warmers
136 Go-To Slipper Socks
139 Go-To Granny Baby Blanket
142 Go-To Chunky Cowl
144 Go-To Chunky Hat

146 **The Contributors**
148 Magana Hi-Low Vest, Paula Pereira
153 Cynnes Anklet Socks, Lydia Gluck

156 Behaaglijk Brioche Cowl, Nancy Marchant
160 Tasche Boho Bag, Drew Emborsky
165 Teas Fair Isle Snood, Tanis Gray
168 Chaleur Cabled Hat, Kate Gagnon Osborn
171 Wärme Mitts, Heather Walpole
175 Calor Chevron Shawl, Marly Bird
178 Hygge Triangle Wrap, Vickie Howell
181 Garam Mukluks, Amy Small
184 Siltums Scarf, Suzanne Middlebrooks

186 **The Knowledge**
188 The Beginnings
193 The Middles
197 The Endings
204 Abbreviations
206 Resources
207 About the Author
208 Acknowledgments

INTRODUCTION

PICKING UP NEEDLES AND YARN HAS BEEN TRANSFORMATIVE FOR ME. IT GAVE ME AN occupation while I was on bedrest, empowered me through a child's chronic illness, and provided a career when I needed it most. After a decade and a half as a professional knitting and crochet ambassador, it's impossible to count all of the miraculous moments I've experienced thanks to yarn crafts. What I *can* do is show the gratitude I feel for those gifts.

For me, you see, life is about showing up—for who and what you love. My way of doing that is by nurturing creativity and encouraging the global knitting community through communication (podcasts, social media, TV series), using yarn as my conduit.

This book is an extension of that showing-upness—a love letter to the craft that feeds my soul, enriches my community, and has opened my world to the possibilities of just how far into this shared life experience that a strand of yarn can take you when you're open to stitching it forward.

XX (<--- Stitch, stitch. ;-)

vickie

ONE

*Profiles, Conversations,
and Community Building with
the Stitcher in Mind*

THE PROFILES

BRISTOL IVY
KAFFE FASSETT
TRISHA MALCOLM
LONDON KAYE
CAITLIN HUNTER
CANDICE ENGLISH
NICKY EPSTEIN
JULIA MADILL
BRITTANY
ERIKA KNIGHT

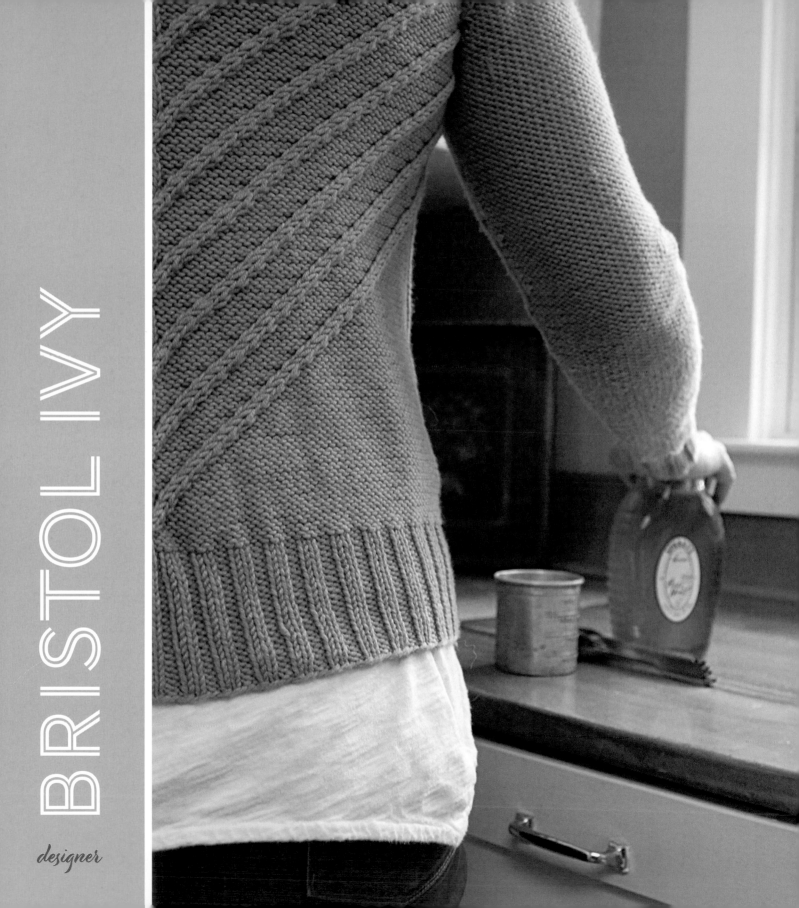

BRISTOL IVY

designer

BY ONE'S OWN DESIGN

BRISTOL IVY is a young, highly skilled designer who is as down-to-earth as she is technically proficient. In her book *Knitting Outside the Box* (Pom Pom Press), she imparts a textbook's worth of knowledge on playing with shape, stitch pattern, and technique. Here, she offers an equally transparent glance into how designers like herself may choose to build a business by stepping beyond boundaries to gain a loyal following.

CREATING A NICHE

In a time when there is so much information, so many options, standing out in any genre can be a challenge. The knitting world is no exception, so many artists are leaning in to very specific niches in order to carve their own distinct place in the community—a strategy that's worked brilliantly for the likes of Nancy Marchant with brioche stitch (see page 156 for her Behaaglijk Brioche Cowl) and Norah Gaughan with cablework. For designer Bristol Ivy, though, it's having a clear voice that defines and draws people to her work. She says, "I think it is incredibly important to have your own aesthetic. Once you develop that, though, you can play within it. The aesthetic brings people to you, because they know what to expect." Ivy continues, "I tend to have a consistent aesthetic in terms of design, and I think people know that I'm going to come at things a little differently than other people might, so they know (with my patterns) it's not going to be a traditional construction or a traditional way to think about historical techniques or something like that. I think that developing [a style] helps build your fan and customer bases."

Bristol is confident in her space, a fact that is reflected in her ability to feel unconstrained by expectations to deliver within the aesthetic for which she's become known. She does, however, acknowledge that there are certain design decisions that don't make sense for her business. "I do know that I have certain things that I can't do as a designer. Like, I couldn't put out a simple top-down raglan sweater and expect it to sell well, because that's not what my audience is looking for. They know they can get that from another designer who has that as part of their wheelhouse. Me doing that would be me being someone else. I don't feel like that reality is confining, I think it's defining."

A LASTING AESTHETIC

So much of the experience of knitting from one of Bristol Ivy's patterns is about the ethos behind it: the way she writes, the way she seems to ponder every stitch. There's a juxtaposition of academic reverence and creative exploration that breathes through the stitches. There's a daring for the knitter to step further. Ivy says, "The biggest thing that I hope people take away from my classes and patterns is agency, in the sense that they're in charge of their own knitting. If they don't want to do something that the pattern says, they don't have to do it. If they want to change a short row technique or if they want to change an increase technique, it's their pattern. It's their garment. It's their piece. It's their knitting. They get to do what makes them happy.

"I studied anthropology in college, and one of the areas where anthropology comes in very strongly with knitting is that in postmodern anthropological theory, there is an understanding that no one person experiences culture the same way as anyone else. Even if we look at the idea of knitting culture, American culture, female culture, there's no set understanding of that. We all have different ways that we view that, and I think the same is true of our knitting history. Our knitting history and what we understand about knitting are so dictated by what we knit, how we knit, the actual physical acts of our hands; all of these things dictate what we see and what we perceive and what we want from knitting." She continues, "I would much rather someone buy one of my patterns, change ninety-five percent of it, and wear it constantly, than buy one of my patterns, knit it exactly to spec, and never wear it. I'd so much rather it be yours than stuck and tied to my artistic interpretation."

Her lasting aesthetic? The ability to lay the foundation for her followers to create their own.

THE MYSTERY OF KNIT-ALONGS

In the days of social media, when we can share progress photos with fellow stitchers worldwide, knit-alongs (KALs) have become an important sales tool for yarn companies who parlay the user-generated WIP (work-in-progress) eye candy into more business. Designers are also using them to sell patterns and to build invaluable community. Those, like Bristol, with a distinct style known by their followers, as well as a reputation for writing solid patterns, are rallying their troops to knit along with them but with an added element of surprise. Mystery KALs are slowly gaining popularity as stitchers take a leap of faith, purchasing designated yarn with a "mystery" pattern, only learning what they will be making as the knit-along progresses. For Bristol, there are benefits and challenges to putting together and running one.

"My philosophy on designers is that there's a spectrum of community involvement. On one end you have people—and this typically is the end that I sit at—where you drop a pattern and there's not a whole lot to do about it," says Ivy. "Maybe you post on social media, but you don't really go past the initial promotion period. On the other end of the spectrum, I think, are the people who produce less frequently but do a lot more community involvement in the [individual] projects, so they're the people who do a knit-along for every pattern. That method involves lots of hand-holding and community support." Finding a healthy balance between those two is something that Bristol likes to pursue in her business, so having knit-alongs, mystery or otherwise, contributes to the goal. For her, it's pushing her out of the comfort zone of simply putting out a pattern and letting it be until the next one is out. It's moving past the model of letting a pattern speak (and sell for itself) and embracing knitters who want more than just a gorgeously designed pattern—they want an experience.

Whereas years ago, Bristol believes, one could walk the grounds at the New York State Sheep and Wool Festival in Rhinebeck and recognize the garments attendees were wearing by the designer behind them, now that's not as much the case. With the advent of Ravelry (the online database and social hub for knitters and crocheters) came the ability for anyone to publish their patterns as a designer, which has resulted in tens of thousands of fish (albeit they may be very different sizes) in a sea in which there used to be a valued few. The community as a whole seems less cohesive, Ivy ponders, "so I think that knit-alongs, and especially mystery knit-alongs, are super important for a designer in terms of marketing, because it is a built-in community right away." The conversation among fellow stitchers, the personal access to a respected designer, and the video and tutorial support that comes with knit-alongs are all key components toward creating that experience.

A CONVERSATION
WITH AN ICONIC DESIGNER

VH: *In 1970, you were working with a fashion designer, Bill Gibb, whose dress was chosen by* Vogue *as Dress of the Year, for which you designed a coordinating waistcoat [see Resources, page 206]. At the time, and arguably still today, knitwear was a sort of stepchild to fashion, and you bringing it in as part of the ensemble and getting acclaim broke barriers for knitting. What was it like to team up on a project like this, and how did you see the industry change because of it?*

KF: Billy was thinking of launching this collection, so I took his drawings to *Vogue* and said, "This is a young genius, just out of art school, and he really should be paid attention to." The editor, Judy Brittain, absolutely got that. She believed. She said, "I've seen your knitting, and I think that if you did a collection with Billy, that that would make it a much more exciting adventure. [You do that and] I will sell that story to a fashion writer." She was working for *Vogue,* so she was obligated to them first and said, "You don't want this story, do you? Because I'm going to take it to the Sunday *Times*." When she did that, *Vogue* told her not to go anywhere else, that they loved the idea and would cover the story.

At this point, I went to Billy and told him that we now had a real chance, that we had the attention of these incredible people. I suggested that we go to the Victoria and Albert Museum and look at Indian miniatures to see how they mixed patterns. Fashion at the time was getting simpler and simpler, pillbox hats, suits, etc., and we thought we could

KAFFE FASSETT is an icon—in the knitting world, in print-making circles, and in the quilting realm. An artist known for his use of color, he's had a career spanning more than fifty years and shows no sign of stopping. I was delighted while speaking with him, via Skype from his European studio, to hear how sharp, passionate, and witty he remains at over eighty years old. It's with good reason that the masses regard Kaffe as textile-world royalty. He's earned it.

KAFFE FASSETT

designer

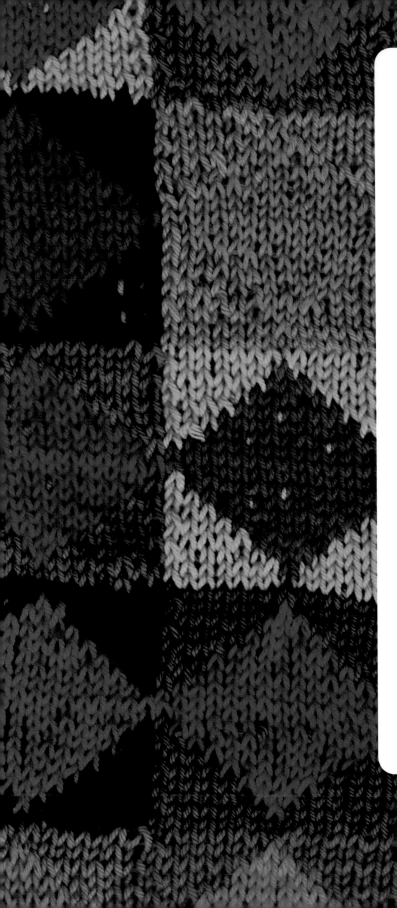

bring some excitement into the period by using those patterns as inspiration. I said, "If you get wonderful tartans from Scotland, and mix that with French flower prints, and then I take that combination, and I pull it together with a piece of knitting that echoes the two worlds coming together, then we have a third pattern story, which makes it incredibly rich. Similar to these Indian miniatures, but uniquely Scottish. He really put his stamp on it. He had a beautiful sense of line and shape in his garments that was just phenomenal from the first go. He was just wonderful.

So he was putting all of that together and won the outfit of the year, because he was the most original voice around. The story was finally covered by the Sunday Times, and they said, this is real handwriting. What a refreshing thing to see, some handwriting.

VH: *Yes, especially, as you said, coming out of the sixties, where there were really not a lot of graphics. The amount of pattern in the outfit that the two of you designed, along with the shape and drape, created something groundbreaking. It wasn't just tiptoeing into redefining style; it was blasting through those boundaries!*

KF: It was very exciting. When you ask what effect that had on the industry, as far as knitting goes, we were pushing the boundaries with machine knitting, too. I was going up to the factory, and working with this guy to produce really beautiful machine knits in incredible colors and spontaneously change the colors in the factory if the first idea wasn't working. I've always worked that way. I like to be spontaneous.

VH: *Were you hand-knitting the samples at that point?*

KF: Yeah, and I was paying very strict attention to how many colors they could do in a row, what the stitch repeat had to be, and so on. I would work within those [machine-knitting] limitations to do the most fabulous thing I could do within that.

VH: *As far as colorwork goes, are there differences between what works well in hand knitting versus machine knitting?*

KF: Yes. with hand knitting, you can bring in a lovely little unexpected color or something. You don't have any limits and you can have as many colors as you want. Even if you reduce it to a few, though, you can put in a little surprise color somewhere, whereas with the machine knitting, there are color repeat rules based on how the machines work. I've had to really sit there and watch the machines and try to understand how we could push the boundaries of them a bit.

VH: *In addition to being a knitter, you're also a weaver, quilter, needlepoint designer, and painter. Is there a difference in the creative space within yourself that each of those individual crafts inhabits, or are they all just extensions of each other?*

KF: Everything I do is an exploration of color. Trying to make colors sexier and more alive and more vibrant or more subtle, whatever it is I'm trying to achieve. I feel like I live in a color lab. Sometimes I place objects together on a table to create a still life, or sometimes I make a collage of fabrics put together to create a patchwork design. Or sometimes I just make a very graphic patchwork or a piece of knitting. Or doing needlepoint stitching, or weaving a tapestry. It's all exploring color. I once read that Bonnard said that a painting, first and foremost, is a beautiful arrangement of color, and then it's whatever subject it is. But that was what was important, and that's what I've always felt is important.

VH: *Was that motivation part of your eventual partnership with Rowan, because of their broad palette?*

KF: Yeah, I think, because when we all first started knitting with Rowan, it was very exciting to be taken seriously and to do big geometric patterns. That was a wonderful period, when we all first started in the eighties, where people were doing some hideous things, you know, great big picture knits and things like that. I wasn't interested in that, but I *was* interested in bringing big brocades and big splashes of color onto people's bodies. Then after a while, I began to realize that a lot of the time, the knitting was kind of wearing the model. You had to be a little more sensitive to bringing out the beauty in the human being rather than overpowering them with something like a billboard.

VH: *You've also done some beautiful black-and-white contrast patterns. I feel like there's nothing like black and white when it comes to crossing genres. The combo is cool and sophisticated; it's chic; it's punk rock. It's a really exciting non-color combination.*

KF: It is very, very exciting. I'm into it more than ever!

VH: *When you were in your late twenties, you were painting, you became interested in textiles, but there was a real stigma against handicrafts and knitting among fine artists. It strikes me that we still see that stigma today, fifty years later. Over the course of your career, have you seen an ebb and flow of that overall mentality?*

KF: I think it's a lot better now. I think when that mad tear-away artist Tracey Emin—the one who was on the 1999 Turner Prize short list for making an installation piece out of her unmade bed surrounded by trash, cigarettes, old condoms, and everything else—put out her knitted designs, it helped [the perception of knitting]. She would knit up great signs and cushions, and she knitted a whole tent, which was another exhibition that went into a museum. And so she brought textiles into the art world and was getting high prices and being taken very seriously. So that was quite a boost for knitting.

VH: *For you, what is the difference between art and craft?*

KF: Well, that's always a fraught question. I would say to people . . . you have to make up your own mind. I'm a painter who's come into the world of using textiles, and I use textiles just the way I use paint. I'm exploring color. I'm exploring pattern. I put as much energy into needlework, and the same kind of thought process, as I would into a painting. So, if they need a label, I leave it to the audience to decide.

"WITH HAND KNITTING, YOU CAN BRING IN A LOVELY LITTLE UNEXPECTED COLOR OR SOMETHING."

LONDON KAYE

street artist

THE DANCE OF AN ARTIST-ENTREPRENEUR

When one thinks of street art, it's pretty safe to say that crochet isn't the medium that first comes to mind. That may be changing, though, thanks to the bold work of artists like **LONDON KAYE**. Inspired by the work of the irreverent Polish crochet artist Olek, but with a decidedly more positive message of color and joy, London's installations add whimsy to the mundane and playfulness to daily life. London gracefully balances on the lines between, then intertwines the worlds of, art, craft, and entrepreneurship.

THE ART OF CRAFT

The difference between art and craft is a much-debated subject within the creative world. For Brooklyn-based street artist London Kaye, who's known for combining the traditional handicraft medium of crochet with modernist installation art, the lines are blurred in definition but clear in application.

"I guess my definition of crafting is 'following instructions.' If you want to learn how to make this particular bracelet, and you go through step by step, you can make it and enjoy your time creating kind of what's laid out in front of you. I suppose my definition of art is organically coming up with the idea, and the concept is all on your own—piecing together your thoughts and your own way of doing things to create something totally unique and different from anything really that has been seen before," says Kaye. Simply put, it's the intent that determines the result. There's craft in art, and potentially art in craft. It's making something out of nothing that transcends characterization.

FOUNDATION. STITCH.

London started crocheting when she was thirteen years old, taught by one of her best friends' moms. Although she studied dance and, growing up, was very active, for some reason, the relatively sedentary craft of crochet stuck with her. Long before she transitioned into street art, she used crochet as a way to relax and also make a little extra money.

"[Crochet] was this one thing that was very peaceful and relaxing, but also I loved it because I would sell scarves to my friends and girls at my dance studio. I loved having my own business and making custom things to sell to people." A born entrepreneur, London was a middle-schooler with a line sheet and a lookbook. She'd carry around a booklet with different yarn colors for people to choose from, then she'd make them a custom scarf. "My first one sold for two dollars. That was in seventh grade. The price raised to maybe around fifteen dollars by the time I was in high school." Over her high school years, she continued selling her crochet wares to individuals and at craft fairs, ultimately earning enough money to buy her first car at age sixteen.

London was raised on a foundation of artistic talent and having a nose for business. Her father is a writer for children's cartoons. One of the influential projects he worked on during London's fifth-grade year was called "How to Make More Than Your Parents." She would travel with her dad to different conventions, learning from him how to promote and sell his work. "It was lots of hustling, but it was really fun for me. I think that's how it all started."

TURNING POINT

Although crochet always lived in the background of her life's story, during her youth, London's true love was dance. A terrible accident in ninth grade kept her off her feet for an entire year, during which she filled her time and kept her connection by crocheting scarves for her dance studio friends. She returned to dance at full steam, however, and was eventually granted a full scholarship in the field at NYU. Due to her injury, she knew that she wouldn't become a professional dancer, but she still embraced the opportunity to follow her passion to perform.

After college London got a job working at the Apple Store. She had always been very techy, a talent that has helped in one of her ventures, 3D-printed crochet hooks. After two years of working at Apple, she decided to take (Apple founder) Steve Jobs's famous advice to follow one's passions. As part of an exercise, she began listing her passions, and crochet inevitably came out toward the top of the list. It was around that point in 2013 when an artist named Olek, whom London wasn't yet familiar with, came into the store carrying an amazing crocheted bag. "Afterwards," London says, "I reprinted her receipt and Googled her name. When I did that I discovered, 'Oh my gosh! You can do more than make scarves with yarn.'" That Google search then led London down a rabbit hole of crochet, during which she stumbled upon yarn bombing. "I always crocheted, so I had a pile of crocheted things in my apartment in Brooklyn. The next day, I took a scarf out of that pile, wrapped it around a tree outside of my house, and instantly was hooked. Literally, hooked."

FROM INSPIRATION TO VOCATION

Since that day, London's work has evolved to include (to name a few) large-scale butterflies, crocheted water flowing from pipes, and a staring blue eye, the latter of which is now iconic to her brand. The motivation for each piece comes from different sources. "When I was first starting out it was just trial and error, anything goes, figuring out new surfaces and simply just doing it. Now that I've been doing [outdoor installations] for about five years, I definitely put more thought into pieces." London now realizes that a piece of art can really affect the community it's displayed in. People notice it, and it plays into their day, so she considers the ramifications of that when she's creating a piece. And people are noticing. Her outdoor works began to gain attention about a month after she started, when people began to reach out to her to create projects for them. It was at the point when Delivery.com approached her to do a commercial for them—a gig that required her to cover two people and an entire room in crochet—that London realized that she could quit her job at Apple and this could be a viable source of income.

CREATIVE SPACE

Other than bringing home the crafty bacon, crochet also continues to fill, in part, London's creative well. While she still takes a ballet class once a week to honor that side of her spirit, it's the act of yarn bombing—creating something, hanging it publicly, then stepping back and watching people take it in—that brings her the most joy. Both dance and street art, however, have a performative aspect to them, a fact that, along with the skills she picked up while working at Apple, underlines for London the evidence that life's experiences along the way help paint a greater picture. To quote Steve Jobs, "Your work is going to fill a large part of your life, and the only way to be truly satisfied is to do what you believe is great work. And the only way to do great work is to love what you do. If you haven't found it yet, keep looking. Don't settle."

TRISHA MALCOLM

editor

A CONVERSATION WITH *VOGUE KNITTING'S* EDITORIAL DIRECTOR

VH: *As the editorial director of* Vogue Knitting, *the largest magazine in the U.S. knitting industry, what are some of the things that you keep in mind when planning an issue?*

TM: We have a formula, in a sense, for what elements make up the magazine. For example, we always cover a yarn store, incorporate some form of travel, and present new products. Having departments that cover each area makes it easier to stay on top of what's up-to-date. In addition, we have articles and what we call "editorial," which is our patterns, and then the instructions.

Patterns are more trend-driven than anything else in the issue. To find those trends, we pull from many, many places. We look at classes that are selling well at our shows. We look at Ravelry, where more knitters hang out than anywhere else. We look at what different influential knitters are doing. And we look at fashion. I spend a lot of time looking through photos of runway shows to see exactly what knits are showing up. This helps us have a sense of what's going to be in stores and what people will be seeing around them. Of course, we are also very interested in what's going on with color, because that's a huge trend unto itself.

TRISHA MALCOLM is a whip-smart, creative, and innovative leader. Not only is she a great wealth of knowledge and invaluable counsel, but I also consider her a dear friend. Over the years we've spent many hours (and bottles of wine) discussing industry issues, strategizing Scorpio (which we both are) world domination, and trading parenting stories. During this conversation, Trisha gives us an insider's look at running a knitting magazine, talks trend-spotting, and shares her views on the evolution of the knitting and crochet market.

"I TRY TO TAKE TRENDS AND TURN THEM INTO SOMETHING THAT'S WEARABLE AND A LITTLE MORE LASTING."

VH: *When you're looking at slideshows of the runway, are you looking at ready-to-wear, high fashion, or a combination of both?*

TM: Combination of both. I research fashion shows in New York, London, Paris, and Milan. I also look at what's going on in Stockholm, Kiev, and Melbourne, just to look, even though they are smaller, but there's a little bit of avant-garde stuff happening there with knit that you aren't really seeing anywhere else. There's some really interesting and innovative stuff, particularly coming out of Russia.

VH: *When you look at avant-garde garments, through the eyes of a magazine editor needing to serve a broader audience, is the goal to translate the off-the-grid looks into something more mainstream? Or is the intention to just create overall balance in any given issue?*

TM: I look it at purely as inspiration. The reality is this: If a knitter spends two to three months making a sweater from our magazine, then we want it to be something that they'll actually wear and that will last. Fashion isn't always wearable or sustainable. For example, there's a missing-sleeve trend happening, but I can't imagine most of our readers would knit a sweater and leave off the sleeve. I try to take trends and turn them into something that's wearable and a little more lasting. Also, our audience consists of different ages, and mostly over forty. Twenty-two-year-olds are not really buying knitting magazines.

VH: *Do you find that the over-forty (mostly) women are open to experimenting a little bit with their knitting? Perhaps trying something with a little nod toward avant-garde, and a bit more out-of-the-box?*

TM: Yes, absolutely. I think that's why we have so many shawl knitters at the moment. Shawls are almost like a blank canvas for anything creative you want to do. Stephen West is a perfect example of someone using the shawl as a playground for color and design-play. Knitters really want to try different and new things: When I look at the classes that our readers sign up for at Vogue Knitting LIVE, for instance, the number of people who have learned to do brioche and entrelac in the last few years is staggering!

VH: *Let's talk about yarn trends. In the twenty years you've been with Vogue Knitting, have you seen certain types or styles of yarn cycle in and out of trend?*

TM: The hand-dyed thing is huge right now, and that wasn't big even fifteen years ago. There was a novelty phase that we all went through. Ruffles, fake furs, that kind of stuff. That was massive. There were also ribbon yarns, which are very hard to find much of anymore, but years ago there were a lot of really great ribbons. Things definitely do trend. Ironically, now when I ask designers about their favorite yarn—right now everyone's favorite is a woolen spun, crunchy kind of wool that does exactly what wool's been doing for the last, you know, five hundred years. A while ago, though, people were into smooth merinos and more processed yarns, but now there's a swing back to a more rustic yarn.

VH: *You've traveled all around the world, and are a native Australian, so you have a broader perspective than most on the integration of knitting into cultures outside the United States. Will you speak to that a bit?*

TM: Everywhere is a little different. There's differences in the way people knit, just for a start, and there are differences in what people knit. In some places they knit utilitarian garments; in others that's less of a focus. There are differences in color, too. Color palettes from the UK (particularly of Rowan and Debbie Bliss) tend to be very different from color palettes from a U.S. company. I don't just mean overall palettes, though. I think just the way colors are varies in different countries. For instance, if you go to Australia, where there is a lot of light, colors tend to be purer and brighter. Compared to a palette from the UK, for instance—Rowan's a perfect example of this, they're more subdued and there's almost like a grain to them. The interpretation of color, particularly in the use of Fair Isle, varies from region to region. Some countries go subtle, others go more graphic.

VH: *Fascinating! What about perception of the craft, though? Much to my chagrin, I still get the "Oh, my nana knits" response from people when I tell them what I do. It's not until I list the books, TV shows, and product lines that are a part of my career that there seems to be a perceived value. Do you feel that knitting is still seen worldwide largely as "women's work"?*

TM: That's an interesting question. I guess that's traditionally what it has been. I can't think of anywhere in the world that it hasn't been that in the last century or so. Particularly when you had two world wars and a lot of people knitted for the war effort. I mean, sure, there were a lot of men who knitted, but in most cases it was the women at home knitting and sending things off to the front. I think that helped make it seem like women's work for several generations. I think that's a really big influence, particularly in the UK and in Australia, and I'm sure in other parts of the world, too. Then, though, we had a generation after, when the hippies embraced making. Then after that, women were more businesslike and in the workforce, so there was less making going on. At that point, handicrafts were shunned by the rising feminism. I think now, though, that shunning mentality is being broken.

VH: *That same feminism is closing the loop; circling back and reclaiming craft.*

TM: Right.

VH: *I think about Debbie Stoller and Stitch 'n Bitch (her groundbreaking series of books-turned-movement) and how that was really the height of reclaiming the craft, but that was fifteen years ago. It sometimes feels like we haven't progressed much, as far as social perception goes. Do you have any insights on what we as professionals in the industry can do to help lift the perception of the value of the craft?*

TM: Yes. A perfect example was when Krysten Ritter was on *The Late Show with Stephen Colbert*. He made a comment about knitting and eighty-year-olds, and she just completely put him in his place by saying, "Look, I'm wearing couture and I'm here making knitting look cool." The celebrity factor has helped before (like fifteen years ago, when *Celebrity Scarves* was published) and continues to do so. Also helping the perception is the information coming out about the health benefits of knitting.

VH: *Yes, the latter is something I'm passionate about [see "The Intention" on page 74]. I think the more that we can align knitting with other practices that have health benefits, like yoga and meditation, as well as place ourselves as a vital part of the maker movement, the better it is for making knitting part of the creative zeitgeist.*

CAITLIN HUNTER

designer

BOYLAND
KNITWORKS

CAITLIN HUNTER has always been a maker. As a child she'd sit next to her mom as she sewed and would use the scraps of fabric to make clothes for her dolls. Later, she would make her sister lie on a piece of fabric and Caitlin would trace her body and then, throwing seam-allowance-and-body-curve caution to the wind, sew the shape into a dress. It wasn't until high school, though, when she was in the basement going through some boxes, that she found an old *Learn to Knit* book. With it, there was some orange acrylic yarn from the 1970s and some plastic needles. It was that day that Caitlin thought, *This looks cool, I'll teach myself to knit.* And then she did.

Coming into her creative self in this free-spirited manner, making it up as she went along, laid the groundwork for some of the colorplay Caitlin would be known for in her future career. Equally important, her fashion design education really cemented her talent for creating beautiful, well-fitting garments.

Caitlin's initial decision to pursue fashion had been a reluctant one. She had always loved making clothing and expressing herself through style, but she was also good in school. She felt torn between her creative hobbies and pursuing something more academic. At the time, she felt that fashion wasn't a serious career. With access to a great program in her native Alaska, she enrolled anyway, and did well.

Her professional life began when she went to work for a menswear and boys' ready-to-wear manufacturer. However, she always kept one foot outside the world of fashion. "I felt uncomfortable with the fast-fashion parts of the profession," shares Hunter, "[It bothered me] knowing that the stuff I was designing was being sold at these mass-market places, like Kmart and Macy's. That they'd be used for a season, then go into a landfill. That they were being produced at these factories in India and China, and polluting the environment, and maybe the people working at these factories weren't being treated as well as they should be." Caitlin was conflicted, though. She loved designing clothing, working with color, and creating things that people could use to express themselves. "It's functional, and art, and I just love that," she says.

After Caitlin met and married her husband, she took a hiatus to raise their twin boys and a third son.

A few years ago for her birthday, Caitlin's mom gave her some nice Rowan yarn: it was a revelation—the first time that she had ever owned, or even seen, a higher-end yarn. She felt like it deserved to be more than an ill-fitting hat, so she went onto Ravelry and settled on the Campside Revisited Shawl by Alicia Plummer. Making that project was the beginning of a love affair with knitting, and the realization that it combined all of her passions for textile, design, and slow fashion. Ready for a new project, she wanted to knit a sweater. When she couldn't find one that she liked, she made one up herself and it clicked: If she got just a little better at knitting, then she could use her design skills in her new craft. And so the ground for her wildly popular knitwear designs and her company, Boyland Knitworks, was laid.

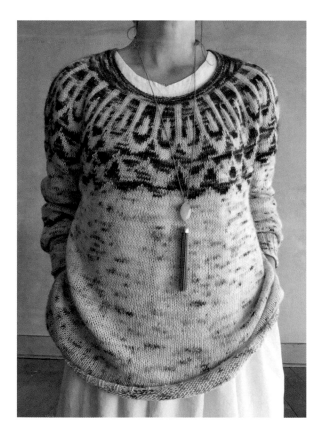

Caitlin Hunter's design aesthetic is very color-driven. Her pieces balance striking graphics with subtle tonal play, and always on a canvas flattering to a woman's body. Her life-long interest in fashion allows for trend-driven origins for her pieces, interpreted in Hunter's unique way. She absorbs trends, then goes with her gut and produces what feels right to her. It's an instinct that has set her apart in the knitting world. For example, when she wanted to keep going with the yoke of a planned sweater design but didn't want to turn it into a cumbersome poncho, the Ravelry-famous Ninilchik Swoncho was the result. "I had no idea it would be so popular," said Caitlin. "I thought maybe a few people would make it if I was lucky. At the time I didn't have a lot of followers, or many patterns out yet. I feel really grateful that I found my people. Knitting just makes us happy, and I feel lucky to be part of this community." Since then, those followers continue to celebrate Caitlin by knitting her designs by the thousands. Her Sunset Highway sweater, inspired by the colors in a palette of Olann hand-dyed yarn, has taken on a life of its own. One would be hard-pressed to visit a knitting convention, wool festival, or yarn store during the cooler months without seeing at least one Sunset Highway making its way down the aisle. Hunter's intent when designing it—to tune in to the knitting community and translate what resonated into a sweater—clearly worked. She wants her designs to be places of comfort for knitters so they feel like there's room for them to express themselves through them. "I just want people to feel free to explore, to change things, to use their own colors, to make [their knitting] a creative outlet. Through my classes and designs, I try to encourage an attitude of enjoyment and relaxation." Caitlin believes that knitting should be fun, and that's the message she wants her classes and colorful designs to share.

A CONVERSATION WITH THE OWNER OF THE FARMER'S DAUGHTER FIBERS

VH: *Your company is called The Farmer's Daughter Fibers. What was life like growing up on a farm, and what type of influence has it had over the trajectory of your career?*

CE: One of the biggest things that I took away from the farm is being hardworking. When you're a rancher, that's all you do. You don't take a lot of vacations. You are up in the middle of the night calving, or harvesting in the summertime; it never ends. I grew up seeing my parents always, always working. And it's not something that's miserable, like, "Oh, I've got to work." It's just what you do and you keep going.

In the last few years, my company has grown so much, but I've put in time and energy, and I love doing it. That tenacity, I think, comes from growing up on a farm.

VH: *That's interesting, and whether you're literally or figuratively cultivating, it all lays the groundwork for skills that are really important to an entrepreneur. What about the influence of the Native American part of your background on your mother's side of the family? Did that part of your culture hold the same, albeit different, weight as the other?*

CE: Yes, it does. It's a really hard thing to explain, though, because it's so intuitive. Its effect is just there. My culture is a huge influence on how I make colorways. I don't go up to a color chart and think, *Oh, this color goes with this,* or *This is a cool color and this is a warm color*. It is all intuitive, and I do think that does come from my Native American culture. It's almost a spiritual thing. The mindset of being present and listening to whatever it is that you're trying to create, then it just kind of flows.

I first encountered **CANDICE ENGLISH**'s The Farmer's Daughter Fibers yarns during a trip to my LYS. I did an about-face when I glanced in the direction of her display, because the use of color was so quietly different from anything I'd seen. I immediately started laying out hanks of her Craggy Tweed to form a gradient of blushes (which later became the Go-To Gradient Scarf; see page 122). I went home and looked up her site, and also fell in love with several colorways of Juicy DK, which would become the first selection in my knitting subscription box business, YarnYAY!

Candice, with her hand-dyed wool as a conduit, exudes a mindful intent that, along with the satisfaction of creating a garment, inextricably makes the stitcher feel purposeful when knitting with her yarns. It's that essence, and the nature-grounded spirituality behind it, that we focused on in this conversation.

CANDICE ENGLISH

yarn dyer

Unfortunately, because my grandparents were taken [as children] and put in a boarding school, a lot of our lines of tradition ended there. We lost so much, but as a family we are trying to get it back. We are very spiritual. My mother in particular tries to connect to our Blackfeet tribal traditions—purely driven by intuition. Listening to self. Listening to nature and listening to the plants.

VH: *Are fiber arts a part of the Blackfeet tradition, or is another type of handiwork more prominent?*

CE: No, fiber arts isn't at all. Beading and leatherwork are more of the handicraft specialties of our tribe. My passion for fiber arts come from my grandmother on my dad's (who's white) side. She did every type you can imagine: macramé, cross-stitch, knitting, crochet. Tons of stuff!

I do, though, use my spirituality to connect with my work dyeing fiber. Our tradition is to light sweetgrass when we pray, or to cleanse a space. I use it a lot of time as a way to clear everything else out of my head so that I'm present and focused on my dye-work.

My mom is an amazing herbalist, and when I first started dyeing yarn, I was using all plant dyes. I knew that I wanted fiber arts to be a part of my everyday life and that I would be able to create a business and make income from it. I also knew that I didn't want to sell fiber that I'd dyed with plants, though, because it is a spiritual thing for me. I'm not buying the dyes. I'm out there, I'm gathering. There's a whole process* in it that I didn't want to profit from.

VH: *Was that your introduction? Did your mom teach you how to dye with plants, or as an herbalist did she simply teach you about the plants and then you experimented with them?*

CE: Exactly. I think just a general knowledge of plants came from her, but it's incredibly hard to find any history of gathering plants to use for dyes. Navajo, I think, you're going to get a lot more because fiber arts are in their tradition, but for us, Blackfeet, you can't find anything. I just kind of, again, make it up as I go, and it is an intuitive thing. You have to, it sounds corny, but listen to the plants. Listen to things. Okay, what about this? What about that? Just being out [in nature], discovering and experimenting.

VH: *When you say "listen to the plants," do you mean like one would listen to their own inner being, or perhaps listen to a spiritual deity?*

CE: I think so. I guess I feel grounded in the area: The reservation borderlines Glacier National Park. Regardless of what you believe, while you're there you can feel something. It's a magical place. It's where I belong. It's where I came from. Maybe it would be like somebody who is Catholic going to Rome—feeling the power of the spirituality.

VH: *We've talked about what guides your personal, natural dyeing. Your colors for your business are so unique, though; will you speak a little to your process for creating The Farmer's Daughter Fiber palettes?*

CE: The dyeing I do for my business is also intuitive. I don't approach a palette looking at what color *needs* to be in it. Or what's lacking. I think what sets me apart is that I try not to think a lot about having a cohesive palette. I focus on something I'm interested in, experiment, then see what feels right. Here's an example: Members of the Mohawk tribe were once a big part of the steel industry and constructing New York buildings. Several years ago, I became obsessed with them. Their families at home were a big part of their story. I was thinking about these Mohawks while I was dyeing and the two came together. I created a palette with this gray steely color, but then there are a lot of blushes and pinks. These men were going home after working for weeks, during which time all they thought about was their families. These blushes and these pinks represent the matriarchs running the homes while the men were away.

When I'm creating a new colorway, it's very much the result of my intention. I don't think that I'd ever found an art besides dyeing in which what I was thinking was transforming my canvas. When I dye, how I feel and what I'm focused on comes through every fiber of the yarn.

See page 94 for Candice's Dye Stuff Harvesting Ritual.

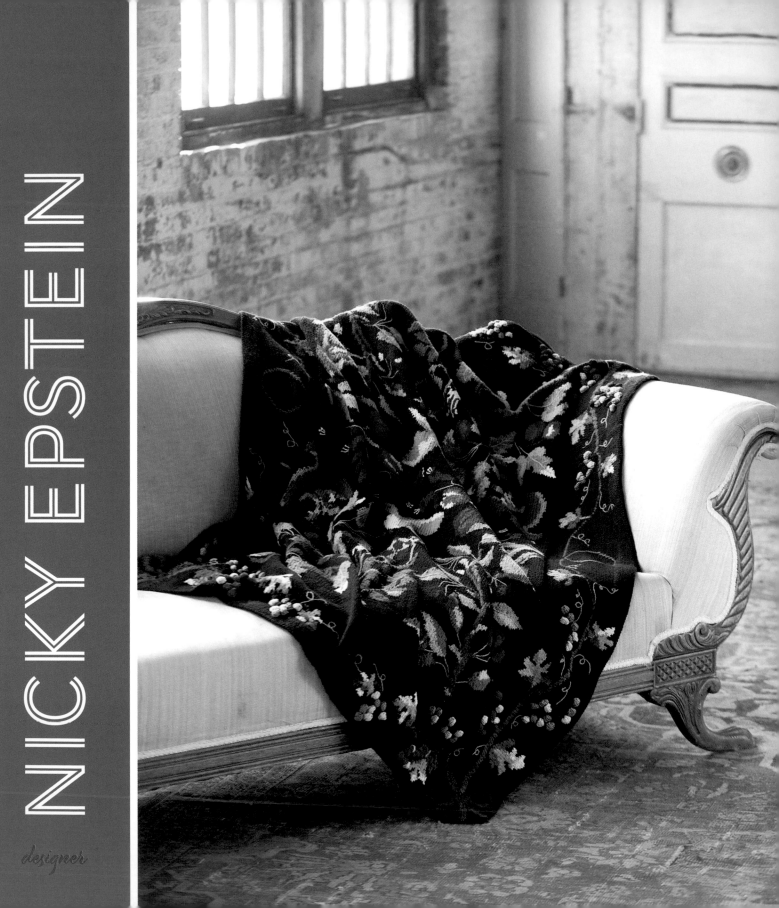

NICKY EPSTEIN

designer

STARTED OFF KICKING!

If you've ever met veteran designer NICKY EPSTEIN, it will not come as a surprise that her plan out of high school was to become a member of the Rockettes. Okay, it might surprise you a little, considering she's all of five feet three inches tall, but what she lacks in height she makes up for tenfold in gumption. (She also, apparently, has great leg extension!) It's that personality, along with a heaping helping of talent, that's fueled a forty-year career as a knitwear designer, author of thirty-plus books, and instructor, and made her a knitting-household name.

Shortly before Nicky was scheduled to travel from her native West Virginia to the New York City audition for an end spot on the Rockettes chorus line, the cousin she was supposed to stay with passed away. Since she no longer had a place to stay, her father wouldn't allow her to travel to the Big Apple, closing the curtains on fulfilling that dream.

Fortunately, dance wasn't the only creative talent Nicky possessed. Nicky had painted since she was a child. With her big-city plans on hold, she decided to move near a friend in Ohio and enroll in the Columbus College of Art and Design. It was there that she learned the usage of color, which would later influence much of the knitting colorwork for which she's so well known today.

ROAD TRIP

After graduating art school, a job as an art director led to a gig doing wardrobe for television (after a fluke opportunity to fill in for a stylist, dressing Humphrey Bogart!), which inadvertently put Nicky on the road toward knitwear designing. On a long trip for work, she realized she was going to be stuck in the California desert for weeks and needed something to keep her occupied. She was traveling in a Winnebago full of men, who gave her five minutes to pick something out at the yarn store she saw on the side of the road. She grabbed a *McCall's* magazine that had an ad for a contest. She'd been knitting since she was six years old, and had the time to create something, so she figured, why not? She grabbed size 2 needles and a bunch of yarn and was on her way to knitting what would become an award-winning unicorn sweater—and a new career!

After winning the *McCall's* contest, the word about her intricate picture-work spread. *McCall's* called *Vogue*, who hired her specifically to do colorwork. It was the early eighties, which in the States meant working with primary colors and acrylics from Monsanto and DuPont, a challenge for an artist trained in a more sophisticated palette, but Nicky remains proud of what she was able to accomplish.

NOW AND THEN

Knitting is cyclical, and Nicky sees certain trends coming and going every cycle. Chunky knits come back around every so often because of the continuous demand for quick knits. Mohair goes in and out and currently is seeing a resurgence. Ombre was a big trend a while back, and has returned under a new, "faded" label. It's all about reviving and renewing. Putting a new spin on an old trend to make it feel fresh again.

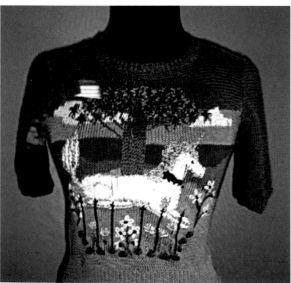

THE MOTHER OF REINVENTION

With thousands of designs published, and hundreds of thousands of books sold, Nicky can add to her talent arsenal the art of reinvention. Over the years she's been the artist of knitted picture work, the designer of avant-garde pieces, and perhaps most strategically during a time when garment patterns are a commodity, the author of staple books on edgings and embellishments. She's designed for the runway and for Barbie dolls. She's taught knitting around the world, while showcasing global stitch traditions in the United States. So how does she continue to keep things fresh? "I love what I do. I've been knitting most of my life, but I still see things I haven't tried before. There are still techniques to be explored, and out-of-the-box ways to apply them. It's so exciting!"

YARNSPIRATIONS

Working for Spinrite (parent company of Patons, Bernat, Caron, and Lily Sugar'n Cream, housed online under the Yarnspirations hub), the largest yarn manufacturer in North America and one of the "Big Three" craft yarn companies in North America, means balancing prolificacy, creativity, and efficiency. Julia does all of that with grace and oh so much style!

I had the pleasure of working with her during some of my time as the international spokesperson for Caron and Bernat, then for Yarnspirations. Years later, I remain in awe of what she and her colleagues are able to accomplish under the constraints of corporate requirements and the insatiable appetite of a knitting and crochet community that always wants more to make with the yarn they adore!

Here's a peek into what it's like to be a driving force behind the style of several major brands.

AN ARTIST AT WORK

Julia attended the Ontario College of Art and Design as an illustration major, a discipline she fumbled her way into under the perception that it would be more practical than fine art. Little did she know then that illustration is a very tough field to make a living in. After years of waitressing and bartending, she eventually landed a job doing motion graphics for television. As time passed, however, she became bored and quit, hoping the need for work would light a fire under her to figure out what she really wanted to do. In the meantime, she took a part-time job at a yarn store, just for fun, while she soul- (and job-) searched. Lo and behold, that led to her current career!

JULIA MADILL may be one of the most well-known designers you've never heard of. As a member of the Yarnspirations design team for more than a decade, she has hundreds of published designs under her belt. Many of those you've likely seen in pattern form as tear-sheets (single, free patterns) hanging near the Patons section in the aisles of JoAnn or Michaels stores, on the ball bands of your favorite Bernat yarn, or even in your own Ravelry queue, including crocheted toys, lace shawls, and graphic Pantone-inspired cardigans. She's one of the talented women who designs them all.

JULIA MADILL

designer

Her training as an artist was not for naught, though. It's a background that has become quite handy for her as a knitwear designer. Fundamentals such as proportion and color theory can apply to almost any creative pursuit and, while in school, Julia also learned creative problem solving, working to deadlines, and how to accept constructive criticism—all crucial skills for a designer.

TEAM WORK

It's not easy to make a hundred-percent living as a full-time designer in the industry. In fact, Julia does it the only way currently possible, by working in-house at an industry company. Although the anonymity of being credited as "Such and Such Design Team" can be frustrating to some, a position like the one Julia's in is coveted by many whose passion for creating outweighs their need for accolades. As Julia says, "You have to let go of your ego if you're working for someone else." In fact, notwithstanding a steady paycheck (a magical unicorn in the life of a knitwear designer), there are many advantages to working on a team that an independent designer doesn't have access to, including support and camaraderie. "One of the major differences [between working on a design team and being self-employed] is that I have a huge support system to help take my design from concept to finished product," says Julia. "My work is test knitted, tech edited, photographed, and laid out for me, which means I can produce many more designs a year than an independent designer. I also *love* working with my fellow designers. We are very supportive of each other and I have learned so much from all of them."

THE PROCESS

As a team, Yarnspirations designers generally collaborate by pooling inspiration and ideas for a collection. From there the designers pick and choose what they'd like to work on individually. Although there are times when a specific request comes through that doesn't speak to any of the designers, Julia says that all in all, "It works out surprisingly well. We know each other's strengths and preferences and are usually pretty fair about it." Julia's favorite projects usually involve a lot of color. The graphic designer in her feeds her love of making charts and diagrams as tools to play around with her ideas.

NEVER A DULL MOMENT

Although there are obvious challenges to designing for four different brands, all of which have different identities and aesthetics, the task definitely keeps the creative juices flowing, and the days interesting! The common consensus of the team is to never assign just one yarn line to any given designer. It would be harder to feel as creatively fulfilled being put in that box. Instead, Julia enjoys the challenge of being a bit of a design chameleon, constantly adapting to a changing set of parameters.

A day in the design office can be very unpredictable. Some days involve Julia just sitting at her desk pattern writing or editing; others involve meetings during which the designers offer input on product expansion, shade card development, and creative direction. Still others may involve appearing in a Facebook Live video or running a photo shoot.

WORKING 9 TO 5

Perhaps the greatest benefit of working for a company, however, is having the ability to set boundaries. Work hours never really end for an independent designer. As a mother to two young girls, Julia feels grateful that she can show her daughters that one can make a living working nine to five creating for someone else, but still take time to feed her own creativity in ways personal to her home, her soul, and her family. Having room to refill one's creative well is a wonderful perk of a job that inspires it.

BRITTANY

designer

B.HOOKED

Whereas designers commonly go to social media to share and promote something they've created, B.hooked's **BRITTANY** (who prefers not to use her last name publicly) got her start as a professional maker, ironically, by not making anything at all. Her public persona grew from a well-curated, niche-specific Pinterest crochet account. She had a clear objective that began with gaining a following based on her eye for detail.

PINTEREST-WORTHY

"[I started with] content curation," shares Brittany, who had researched other crochet accounts and surmised that the biggest issue with them was that there were often broken links or misdirected URLs. As crafters, not being able to find the pattern for something we want to make can be frustrating. For Brittany, it's a pet peeve, and one she thought she could use to her advantage. She thought, *If I can be the one account that makes sure that every single thing that I re-pin goes back to where it's supposed to, then that's my secret sauce.* And so it was. She created many different crochet-centric boards and made them all distinct. If someone was looking for a baby's hat or Thanksgiving crochet patterns, for example, Brittany had boards tagged with those terms and they all linked back to where they were supposed to. Through that practice, she herself became a reliable source.

As she enjoyed every aspect of running a website—from graphic design and photography, to writing tutorials—Brittany knew that was the direction she wanted to go. Once she built an audience on Pinterest, it was time to give them someplace of her own to go. B.hooked, the home base for Brittany's designs, videos, podcasts, and tutorials, was born.

BUT FIRST, GET HOOKED

Brittany wasn't always a crocheter, but she came from a family filled with creative types so she was always open to exploring craft. It was after she met her husband during her senior year in a pre-med program college, however, that her life changed direction to one that would eventually lead to her picking up a hook. She no longer wanted to go to medical school and was working in a lab; suddenly, without an intensive study schedule filling her evenings, she found herself with free time. She was bored to tears. She needed something to occupy her hands. She once joked with her husband, "I'm going to go to Hobby Lobby, and I'm coming back with a hobby." She went to the store and stayed several hours. She looked at all of the hobby options, weighing the pros and cons, and ended up in the yarn aisle. Being there sparked a memory of her grandmother who, before she passed away, crocheted. She thought, "The yarn fiber arts, that has a real potential. It seems portable. It's super affordable, and I can get really creative with it." She was drawn to the colors and different textures of all the yarns, and she was excited about the prospect of making something for her sister's baby-to-be. The opportunity to create with yarn felt endless! After some experimentation with different yarn crafts, she took to crochet. She jumped on YouTube to learn the stitches, and the foundation for her new hobby-cum-career was laid.

THE B.HOOKED METHOD

At its heart, B.hooked is a resource for learning crochet and knitting. Brittany herself claims to have a unique learning style which, during her time in college, led her to develop a theory on adult learning that she applies to her very specific way of teaching today. "Adult learning theory, to me, is that adults learn best by doing." Brittany posits, "One of the things I found in learning how to crochet and knit on YouTube is that people were constantly showing me what to do, and that was really helpful. I can typically pick up and follow right along with them. The disconnect for me though, was that I was never being taught *why* I was doing what I was doing. Understanding the 'why' behind those things is kind of the bridge for that higher level of understanding."

Much like with the organizational need for crocheters on Pinterest, Brittany saw a systems change that could benefit stitchers on YouTube. She knew she wasn't the only crafter who had an analytical approach to things. That was her angle in starting her YouTube channel and inadvertently developing her teaching style. "I teach in the way that I learn," Brittany states. She feels a responsibility to tap into the community's need for knowledge. She logically anticipates the questions that might naturally come up when any particular topic is taught and listens to her audience for exactly the information they want to gain. A culmination of data from that process propels her videos and podcast tutorials.

Brittany shares, "By watching and listening to the community, I have figured out that there's a paradigm in the questions. The biggest trend in questions that I see coming through are definitely pattern related, and the assurance of whether or not they're doing it right. The assurance part is a little bit more difficult to address because there's not necessarily a question to answer. It's more about assuring stitchers that X is the end goal, and whether you take route A, B, or C to get there, the only thing that matters is that you get to point X."

To further her point, Brittany created a ten-part podcast series that addresses the technical aspects of reading a crochet pattern, as well as how to deal with some of the mind games that we stitchers play with ourselves. Through that series she intends for listeners to get past the barriers that prevent them from reading patterns and to give them the confidence they need to succeed.

What's the endgame to Brittany's method? "There's a real joy that comes from knitting and crocheting, and it's more than a hobby for a lot of people." Brittany considers, "It's a real shame to come to a point in your stitch work where you're stuck and you have nobody to help you out from that. I hope to be the person to educate them, inspire them, and to continue that relationship, and help them in the ways that they need help." In the end, what she does is nurture joy.

A CONVERSATION WITH A PIONEERING BRITISH DESIGNER

I've said it before, I'll say it again. **ERIKA KNIGHT** is my design-spirit animal. Her designs, yarn lines, and books all manage to find the sweet spot between simple but interesting and classic but cool. I met her for the first time in 2005 when she was a guest on a show I used to host, *Knitty Gritty,* and since then I've had the pleasure of working in her orbit every now and again. Erika's witty, creative, and so much fun. At the heart of what makes up the treasure that she is, though, is her true love of creativity. That spirit is contagious. We focus on her punk-rock past in this conversation, because, well, Erika's the coolest!

VH: *In your designs you often play with contrast. You use neutrals, often laying blacks, whites, and grays against pops of magenta, pink, and red. Your career in fashion began around the time of the British punk emergence and right in the middle of John Lennon going out on his own. When I think of John Lennon and his movement, I think of nice, neutral colors. When I think of Sid Vicious and the Sex Pistols and the Cult, I think of blacks, and whites, and reds, and pinks. I wonder if that period of time, culturally, musically, and politically, laid the subconscious groundwork for your use of color?*

EK: I love the way you actually put that, Vickie, because I think with all creativity it's not just in isolation, it's not just about what sort of genre creativity we do. For me it's always about scooping up what's around you. I was at art school during that time [you mentioned] and the one thing I knew was the world wasn't waiting for a fairly mediocre painter. What was fantastic, though, was that I studied painting. It was a very "Bomberg" type of school. It's all about color and expressionism. There I was doing silk screens with sixty-four colors and not going over the edges, and making it very influenced by that fabulous Frank Stella. Then I thought, you know, *I am a person who goes over the edges. I've got to get messy again*. So, I went back to basics, and Robert Ryman again, it was all about whites and a million shades of whites and texture. Maybe I'm just a true Gemini: I'm color on one hand (the simplicity) and tones of a color on the other hand.

What was also fantastic about that time was being surrounded by fashion. We'd club seven nights a week, and we'd work seven days a week. [The vibe] was [Sex Pistols singer] Johnny Rotten, and it was Kraftwerk, which I think

"I THINK THE MUSIC
WE ALL KNIT TO
IS A SOUNDTRACK
TO OUR CREATIVITY"

should be my signature. At that point, I just knitted for friends. They couldn't knit, so I interpreted their collections and made some knits, and threw them down the runway to the soundtrack of my generation.

VH: *You were creating knit pieces for people in bands?*

EK: We did do knit pieces for the people in bands. When I was at college it would be for friends and would-be up-and-coming designers, of which there have been many. But certainly, even during the eighties with Band Aid, I think I can still stop the video and look in the background and about two or three of them are wearing our sweaters. That was quite a thrill as well. I'm all style over substance, Vickie. I have embraced every youth culture from Mod to Punk to New Romantic and I think the music we all knit to is a soundtrack to our creativity. People have said that knitwear sort of dipped in the eighties, but I found those years to be very creative. On the one hand, we were taking influence very much from Japanese designers and deconstructing and putting outside seams on the knitwear. On the other, we were influenced by French spinners like Phildar and American pop culture, like [TV shows] *Dynasty* and *Dallas*. Our pieces were loud, out-there club pieces. We did this one little clubby vest design, knit with exposed seams and leather lacing, that got noticed by entrepreneur Joseph Ettedgui, who dominated the eighties British fashion scene. He ended up ordering them to be carried in his fabulous shop. After that they really took off! We had so many to make, there wasn't time for clubbing!

VH: *When you say "we," does that mean you had sort of your own little street force?*

EK: I live on the South Coast in the UK and I had, at that time, about a thousand outworkers—a thousand cottage industry people knitting and making ready-to-wear for shops all over the world.

VH: *How did you find all of those workers? Nowadays you can put a call out on Twitter or Ravelry. That wasn't an option then.*

EK: Back then we relied on old mail. We put out a little ad. It was a way for me to harness the talents of the most amazing women. Some of these stitchers couldn't always go out to work, or maybe they could but just needed a few pounds more in their wage. There weren't the opportunities that there are now. This work gave them creativity. It gave them economy. It gave them socialization. And I learned all the techniques of the trade through these wonderful women who, given a different opportunity of time, and industry, and Etsy, and Ravelry, would have captained industry. They were amazing.

VH: *One of your more recent projects is another retail collaboration with the London-based John Lewis. Here in the U.S., craft being showcased in a department store seems like a pipe dream. Is there more of an openness to the value of DIY in the UK?*

EK: The John Lewis haberdashery department has always been a destination for fabric, yarns, and everything happy. Knitting is so popular now that I think it's them being very proactive, teaming up with someone like me. People are willing to give knitting a go, so the fact that retail and the industry, in a really properly commercial way, can embrace what we as crafters do, I think is exceptional. Part of my ethos really, and I know it is for you, Vickie, too, is to make craft with a big "C." Not with a small "c," so the industry takes it seriously.

VH: *I'd love to end this piece with a quote from you from your book* Simple Color Knitting, *because for me, it really encapsulates your message as a leader in our community.*

EK: Absolutely. "We must hold on to our individuality through our creative endeavors, most especially our handknits. Key to this is the handcrafted. A craft that comes from the hand is, for me, the greatest form of creativity, honest, authentic, and personal."

THE COMMUNITY

Whether it be a physical item that symbolized a movement, a personal struggle conquered, the drive to create a better culture for others, or the life-purpose to publicly share beauty and light, the effects of hand-making resonate across our community and beyond.

KNIT COLLAGE
INDIAN CO-OP
THE WELCOME
BLANKET PROJECT
THE PUSSYHAT PROJECT
BRINI MAXWELL &
JOSH BENNETT
THE EMILIO
SCARF PROJECT
SIEDAH GARRETT
ELISABETH WARD
THE KNIT HIVE

KNIT COLLAGE INDIAN CO-OP

AMY SMALL

Amy Small got her start as a sweater designer for Bohemian-chic retailer Free People. It was a dream job, giving her the opportunity to learn at different factories all over the world and to travel, as well as introducing her to the handspun yarns that would later inspire the launch of her business, Knit Collage.

She and one other woman were in charge of sweater design at Free People. Amy's specialty garments were lovingly called "kitchen sink" sweaters because they had a lot of things going on, such as colorwork with beading, embroidery on top, and a different placket and cuffs. These were defining pieces for the business at the time.

Unlike other teams within Free People, hers traveled quite frequently. Her boss felt she could create and design the best work at the factories, because with yarn, you're creating your own fabric. So much can change, like the gauge or the stitch or the colorwork. Being there, versus at a desk in an office, meant that Amy could experiment with the yarns. She could play.

During her time in India for work, she realized there was a whole world of art yarns and beautiful things that could be made on a spinning wheel. Amy learned how to spin, and it became more than a hobby for her. It was her passion. She also fell in love with the colorful textiles and the Indian culture.

A series of events moved her to Hong Kong, where she decided to go freelance. She had U.S. and Chinese contracts designing sweaters for factories that would then sell to bigger clients. At the same time, she noticed that the types of yarns she wanted to see just weren't in the marketplace.

She began to spin her own yarn, creating a small collection of what would become Knit Collage's Gypsy Garden yarn. A friend of her parents owned a yarn store and suggested Amy go to TNNA (the industry market convention, hosted by the National Needle Arts Association.) She did, and Knit Collage was born.

With a new business to run, Amy had to figure how to get the yarn made. She couldn't fulfill orders by spinning everything herself. For a time, she worked with women she recruited to work with her at a studio in Hong Kong. Ultimately, though, she wanted to be back in India and support women and craft there. Women in that region are amazing at handwork. Everyone works really hard and is inherently ingenious. Amy wanted her yarns to look like they were made by hand. To include trims and many colors. To be unique. It was going to be difficult to pull off, but less so in that culture with so many remarkable materials available.

Amy's former Free People boss still lives in India part-time and helped her get set up. She then partnered with a woman she had also previously worked with (during a stint at Free

People's sister company Urban Outfitters), who helped Amy find the right ladies to spin, figure out where to get different trimmings, and to manage the studio while Amy (who had met and married her husband and moved back to the Boston area) ran operations in the States.

During her sweater design days in India, one thing was very apparent to Amy: There weren't any women in sweater factories. That was due in large part to the fact that they were viewed as unreliable labor sources because they had children and domestic duties. In developing her own workforce, it was really important to Amy to find and be able to support women who wanted work. She created a co-op of thirteen incredible women, twelve of whom have been with her since the beginning, including three generations of one family.

The spinning technique is different in India than elsewhere, however, and Amy found that it wasn't resulting in the fibers she wanted. She trained her team on the basics of working on a spinning wheel and then the women took it from there. At this point, Amy says, their skills surpass her own.

Now a mother to two small boys, Amy goes to India twice a year to design the season's collections. She chooses trims, conceives yarn designs, approves labels, and gets the ball rolling on production. She also makes the pilgrimage to refill her cup. For upcoming seasons, she and her team might play with tie-dyeing cotton or hand-painting chiffon, figuring out how it might translate into a Knit Collage yarn. Being around the co-op invigorates her and reminds her of her purpose: to produce beautiful, artful fiber while supporting other creative, hardworking women.

JAYNA ZWEIMAN

WITH OPEN ARMS

I started working on the idea of the Welcome Blanket Project, an organization that provides handmade blankets to refugees, as a response to Donald Trump's candidacy announcement back in 2015. As a grandchild of immigrants, as a friend of immigrants, and as someone who has loved working abroad in other countries, I could not believe the amount of vitriolic xenophobia Trump spewed. I wanted to challenge Trump's views, and to provide a space for Americans to choose how we want to behave as individuals and a society. Though the United States has a history of treating the newest wave of immigrants with suspicion, we can—and must—learn from our past mistakes.

What makes the United States great is our pluralism and diversity. Support of immigrants is crucial to our country's identity: each person has a story of immigration, migration, or relocation. We must have productive conversations about immigration, while showing kindness to our newest neighbors, so they know that they, too, belong.

Through the blankets and the welcome notes, participants not only provide tangible gifts of warmth, but also share their own immigration stories, connecting their personal histories to this current complex issue of immigration. It makes the political personal. It helps create our country's collective story.

Through this initiative a powerful village has risen. The strength, creativity, and intensity of the Welcome Blanket community has been inspirational. So many people care deeply about immigration and asylum. They are looking for a positive and practical way for their voices to be heard. Creating a platform for participation and productive conversation is possible and necessary. I want to do everything I can to foster that.

JAYNA ZWEIMAN is the founder of Welcome Blanket and the cofounder of the Pussyhat Project. She holds a master's in architecture from the Harvard University Graduate School of Design, training that she often uses when considering the application of fiber to structure and space. She lives in Los Angeles, California.

Throughout my career, I have been interested in knitting as an abstract idea about lines (of yarn) becoming surfaces and objects. As soon as the idea for Trump's border wall was announced, I couldn't understand that distance conceptually, so I thought about how long it might take to knit it. Welcome Blanket took off from there.

Beyond my professional design focus, my own family's history is the motivation for Welcome Blanket. All four of my grandparents immigrated to the United States (one as a refugee), and I am the product of the American Dream.

My grandfather would never talk of his long journey by boat—only the moment he saw the Statue of Liberty. Then he would smile, eyes lit up, and sigh, "After eight years waiting, I saw the Statue of Liberty . . . and I knew I made it."

My grandparents sought opportunity, safety, and freedom here in the United States. They laid the foundation for my family in this country through hard work, integrity, and kindness. I think my grandparents would be proud of this project. It's because of them that I can even create Welcome Blanket. They paved the way for me to feel at home, to follow my path wholeheartedly, to make a positive difference—here in the United States.

I live in Los Angeles, one of the most diverse and complex—and dynamic—cities in the world. Many of my friends, neighbors, and family are immigrants, some are refugees. When I meet people in L.A., I often end up talking about immigration. I get around the city in ride shares and I meet drivers from all over. I have the privilege of asking about and listening to their stories. Many are immigrants, children of immigrants, or grandchildren of immigrants. We talk about our shared fear of how people who came here to make a better life are being treated.

As we debate methods and numbers concerning immigration, it's important to remember we are talking about real human beings: people like ourselves, our neighbors, and our ancestors. To remember the humanness is to remember that each person arriving in the United States has value.

I see my grandparents in the people who, at this very moment, are trying to come to the United States. I want to welcome our newest neighbors with the same opportunity, safety, and freedom my grandparents hoped for. You, dear stitcher, can help me do that.

HOW TO GET INVOLVED

The proposed border wall between the United States and Mexico is almost 2,000 miles long. Imagine if the massive distance of this wall were reconceptualized and recontextualized not to divide, but to include. Instead of wall, a concrete line, to keep people out, what if lines of yarn became 3,500,640 yards of blankets to welcome people in?

Welcome Blanket is a three-stage powerful, positive process:

1. Making the Welcome Blanket/writing the note on one's own or in a group.

2. Coming together and showing these gorgeous works as a collective statement of action.

3. Gifting Welcome Blankets and notes to personally connect and support our new neighbors.

By using our needles and hooks, we make ideas and concepts visible and relatable. And we more openly relate to each other.

To be a part of Welcome Blanket, craftivists can create and donate a 40" x 40" blanket along with a personal message of welcome to immigrants (see the Resources section on page 206 for site info; donation locations vary). These packages are collected and displayed at host museums. After shows close, the blankets are distributed to refugee resettlement organizations. I hope these Welcome Blankets become powerful symbols for the people who will be receiving them. I hope that the ideas and ideals of "life, liberty, and pursuit of happiness" are transmitted.

It takes a lot of time and effort to create a blanket. The intricacy and dedication seen through the blankets (either on our online gallery or at a physical installation) are incredible. You can feel the history of someone's hands in a handmade Welcome Blanket. The love is palpable.

THE PUSSYHAT PROJECT

Photo of Krista Suh by Rachael Lee Stroud

KRISTA SUH

Wanting to make a huge statement at the January 2017 Women's March, Krista Suh realized that making protest gear with her own hands would be meaningful. A beginner obsessed with knitting, she realized *she* could actually make her own hat. It was a big moment. Then she thought, if *she* could make this hat, anyone could! That's when her vision of a protest hat went from one to many—she could *see* the sea of pink that an army of women could create. She knew that if she made a pattern and shared it, knitters everywhere would be eager to take up the "call to arms," taking a stand through a medium they loved. Thus the Pussyhat Project (TPP) was born.

THE MOVEMENT BEGINS

From the moment of inception, Krista Suh knew TPP would be huge. She was in the backseat of her parents' car when she dreamed up the idea that one hat could be an inspiration to many, and immediately texted Kat Coyle, designer and owner of her local yarn shop, the Little Knittery (Southern California). Krista also teamed up with would-be co-founder Jayna Zweiman (see also page 53), whose architectural training and experience with events were crucial to the development and launch of the project. The excitement their idea spawned, for everyone in the shop that day, when all of the TPP pieces fell into place, was palpable. They'd hoped and planned from the beginning that it would be bigger than even Krista's imagination could conceive. It was indeed.

THE DREAM BECOMES REALITY

The hope was for marginalized people to come together in a big, bold, fearless way to show that they are not invisible. That they're not going away. Women, people of color, liberals, progressives, LGBTQ people—the collective was angry and ready to speak up. Inherently and importantly, TPP was a way for people to participate in the Women's March, even if they could not be there in person. The act of making something with your hands is a deep show of support. The act of giving your creation away to another person, who then makes a stand by wearing it proudly, is a powerful show of unity. Everyone involved was a (s)hero.

THE COLOR THAT SPLASHED A NATION...AND BEYOND

Krista chose the color pink because she didn't want to shy away from what was stereotypically considered feminine. Historically, at least over the past century, pink, with its association with the female sex, has been considered a symbol of weakness. Ironically, that wasn't always the case. Since pink is in the red family—a palette traditionally associated with war, strength, and power—it was originally partnered with the male sex. At one time blue was considered demure, oceanic, calm (read: weak), and peaceful (for example, the Virgin Mary wears blue). It wasn't until the early 1920s that the gender associations of both pink and blue began to shift, and swap places. Then, according to Jo B. Paoletti, historian and author of *Pink and Blue: Telling the Boys from the Girls in America,* the line was firmly drawn in the 1980s when it became commonplace to learn the gender of one's baby before birth, and the rise in popularity of toys like Barbie and non-gender-neutral clothing, in response to the drabber, post–World War II period, seemed to seal the deal. Pink was for girls. Girls were the weaker sex. There you go.

Krista reclaimed the color's association with strength by choosing pink for the Pussyhat.

WHY THE PUSSYHAT?

From the beginning, Krista wanted the hat to have cat ears. She felt the silhouette was interesting and would stand out in a crowd of beanies with a pom-pom on top. Having two points instead of one was eye-catching and effective. But then there was the question, "What is the meaning of cat ears?" The question was posed, during that same yarn shop meeting. At first, there was silence, until Kat Coyle spoke up: "It's the pussy power hat!" The perfection of that was so clear. "We knew that was it. So it was pink, it had cat ears, and it was called the Pussyhat."

THE PUSHBACK

The project, arguably due to the irreverence of the name, wasn't well received by all women, though—some took the name literally, thinking the hat was supposed to represent a vulva, and brushed the movement aside as a global act of vulgarity. Yarn shops across the United States, Australia, Canada, and the UK could be found donating pink yarn and encouraging customers to come in to knit their Pussyhats in solidarity. At least a couple of store owners, however, were unamused. One even refused to sell pink yarn to customers who intended to use it to make a Pussyhat.

Regardless of which side you landed on, though, there was one undebatable fact: yarn now held a new power. Krista was surprised, and yet not surprised at all, at those women who were offended by the Pussyhat Project. She believes that everyone has their own feminist journey, processing in their own way. It's upsetting, however, to realize how deeply patriarchy impacts our lives in even the smallest moments. She wants women to know, even those who don't understand or are offended by the project, that the Pussyhat is intended to be an object of empowerment for all women.

A VOICE FOR MODERN FEMINISM

There's a certain level of responsibility that someone with a large voice might shoulder, and Krista definitely feels the call to continue creating progress in unique ways that bring in more people. She sees herself, in part, as the feminist welcoming committee. Before the experience of founding TPP, she used to be afraid of the political process. After being thrust into it, she sees that it's not so scary after all. She

strives to encourage other women to join in and speak up. In her book *DIY Rules for a WTF World,* Suh talks about the difference between scary and dangerous. It might be scary for many to speak up (whether it is speaking up at a town hall, in a knitting circle, or in your own family), but it is so important because by speaking up, we make it less fearful for others. We also speak up for people for who can't do it themselves, because of the risk of dangerous consequences. To Krista, patriarchy is not about man vs. woman, or even masculine vs. feminine. It's about the false idea that there's one right way of doing something, and if you're not a part of the ruling class (rich white male), then that way is wrong. Creativity, craftivism, and yes, knitting are the antidote to patriarchy because they prove to and remind people that there are many ways to do something. The way that you, as an individual, choose to do it is valid.

BEYOND THE PUSSYHAT

Before TPP, Krista hadn't before used knitting as a vehicle of protest. Knitting then was more of a vehicle for relaxation, fun, and meditation. However, she's always used clothes and art as a means of communication. She has a background in film and event producing, so her work now combines all of her favorite things to make a statement for causes she passionately believes in. Women's liberation is her life. Post-TPP she continues to lean into that liberation by being a voice for it among knitters, crocheters, and young women.

Following the Pussyhat Project, Krista embarked on the Evil Eye Gloves campaign, intended to bring more eyes onto the dire state of gun violence the United States is in. This project started out as a dream Suh had of thousands of women coming together peacefully, with their hands in the air, and on each hand an evil eye was painted. She knew that was a powerful image but wasn't sure how it would be realized until the Pussyhat took off and she thought, *Oh my God! Of course! We could knit these!* Whenever we knit, we are infusing what we make with love, and the Evil Eye Gloves are a symbol of protection, a gift of the wish for safety that we are giving to the wearer, even if the wearer is a stranger.

Krista loves that knitting took the world by surprise, and yet, longtime knitters are not surprised at all by the community and the fervor knitters have. We are strong. We are united.

Photograph of Brini Maxwell and Josh Bennett by the Drunken Photographer

HANGING OUT WITH THE CLUB CUMMING KNIT@NITE HOSTS

I sat down with my friends style personality Brini Maxwell and knitwear fashion designer Josh Bennett to catch up on the evolution of an unlikely regular event that they cohost, a knit night at a celebrity-owned cabaret club on the Lower East Side of Manhattan. We talk about the power of inclusivity, how to keep things entertaining, and what keeps people coming back week after week to bask in the quirky glory of Knit@Nite at Club Cumming.

VH: *Knitting has been known for stitching bees, stich 'n' bitch groups, and gatherings since the beginning of knitting time, but Knit@Nite (hosted at a club owned by gender-fluid actor Alan Cumming), opens some unexpected doors for the craft.*

JB: Long before Knit@Nite, I'd taught Alan [Cumming] how to knit. We'd met years before at a cabaret show at the Supper Club in the King Kong Room, which doesn't exist anymore.

BM: I had done a couple of events at Club Cumming with Michael Musto and my name came up as someone who would be a good fit for doing this knitting event, because of my television show [*The Brini Maxwell Show*, Style Network], which had domestic tips, recipes, craft projects, and the like.

VH: *Were you a knitter at that point?*

BM: Not yet, but I had done other sorts of fiber crafts, like embroidery. I'd also had Debbie Stoller [*Bust* magazine, author of the *Stitch 'n Bitch* book series] as a guest on an episode of my show focused on Colonial America. During the segment we talked about the relationship of needlework to women, the women's movement, and how women's work became the glue that held the community together.

The combination of those experiences made me a good match for this particular project. Josh was brought in as the high-profile knit pro for what was supposed to just be one night, but he thought the event was interesting and signed on to cohost.

VH: *Did you know each other before that?*

BM: No. We met at the first Knit@Nite in October 2017.

JB: Alan mentioned a knitting night at the club in a *Lonely Planet* article and it kind of blew up without planning anything. They wanted someone good with a mic, but also needed knitting instruction.

BM: The intention was to have an event that was entertaining, in addition to being about knitting.

JB: Yes. We wanted to be able to teach knitting, but we're at a place with a stage so there should be a show aspect to it. Other than your show [*The Knit Show*], Vickie, there isn't any other venue to interview craft people live, drink, and do fun, silly games.

VH: *So, Knit@Nite is almost like an interactive variety show? With knitting.*

JB: Yes, or with a talk-show vibe.

BM: Yes, it does have that quality of a confessional.

VH: *When I was there, I think it was only the second event, so I don't think that was yet the format. What does an evening with you two look like now?*

JB: An intimate atmosphere with drinks. It's more casual. You can knit. You can not knit. You can drink. You can just pretend to knit. You can do anything, but you don't have to do anything. I think that's very important, that if you just wanna come see a show about craft or fiber, you don't have to bring your stuff with you. You can just have a good two hours.

BM: Another thing that has become really special about Knit@Nite is our regulars, who all know each other and come to that event specifically to see each other, in a lot of cases.

JB: We have open seating, so people can come in when the doors open at 6 p.m. and get situated. I always love when new people come in and they have to sit at a table of regulars. Everyone makes friends. Then around 6:30 or so, we go up onstage and give a twenty-minute presentation. We show off Brini's outfit, talk about our week, and then transition into raffle giveaways. Then, we either have a guest or play a game. We wrap up just before 8, with another raffle and teasing next week's event.

BM: In between all of that, though, we're very active among participants. We go from table to table, ask people what they're working on, talk to them about what they've been doing during the week, introduce new people to make connections. We really do act as hosts, in a traditional party kind of way. Making people feel comfortable and at ease, I think, accounts for some of the success of the night. We create an atmosphere of comfort and ease and camaraderie.

JB: I also see this as something we can take on the road. We can come host knitting nights. No one's really doing anything like that. I think it's fun, and it makes me excited about knitting again, just being around knitters.

VH: *I agree. Your presentation is very unique. I'm also not aware of other knitting events that are as inclusive to the LGBTQ community as this one. Is that inclusivity part of what you hope to bring to the overall knitting community? Or is that really just a sidebar?*

JB: I think it's just a side effect. I mean, Club Cumming is so inclusive and it's really about a bar for everybody, and quirky performances and you can be yourself there. The space already lends itself to being inclusive because Alan specifically created that kind of cabaret space. I love it that we have everyone there. We're pretty much the United Colors of Benetton of the knitting world.

BM: There's a very welcoming quality to Club Cumming from the point of view of being a gay bar that is designed to make everyone feel at home and comfortable in it.

VH: *What I found really fascinating when I was there was the diversity of the group. Straight, gay, young, older, white, Asian, female, male, you name it. It sounds like you're getting a lot of that type of traffic—people who want to be a part of whatever that essence is. What do you hope the takeaway is from their time at Knit@Nite?*

JB: The regulars have become like a family to us. I miss them when I'm traveling and can't be at Knit@Nite. I want them to feel that.

BM: Yes. We just want them to leave with a sense of belonging, really. That would be at the top of my list. I want people to feel like they are welcome, that there are like-minded people there, and that they can come back as often as they like and there will always be a place for them there.

DIVA ZAPPA

Actress Diva Zappa (daughter of legendary musician Frank Zappa) started crocheting, then knitting, much in the way she's been raised to live her life: unconventionally. Whereas many learn to make things by following instructions, after a quick lesson from actress Laurie Metcalf, Diva grabbed supplies and just started making. Her knit and crochet creations started without expectation and transformed at her fingertips into whatever they wanted to be, which could be anything from an asymmetrical hat to a dress fit for (and worn by) a red carpet–bound rock star's wife. Her pieces were the poster projects of free-spiritedness. They were the bits of frayed crepe paper and glittery string that might adorn the box most of us craft within.

Diva learned to read patterns so that she could have a better understanding of directional knitting but really, that was just a formality. The project would always be what it wanted to be, regardless of practice.

One day, about a decade ago, her knitting decided it wanted to go in one direction, that of growth. It was the beginning of a knit that may (or may not, depending on where it leads her) become Diva's life's work. A few rows turned into more, and then more, and the Emilio Scarf Project began.

Unusual for Diva, this project knew exactly what it wanted to be from the get-go. "Emilio, when he was . . . sorry, I talk about him like he's a person, because he's going to be with me for a very long time," Diva notes, "when he was liter-ally two inches long, the piece spoke to me and was like, 'My name is Emilio, I'm going to be a scarf, and I'm going to be a mile long.' I was just like, Okay, let's do this," Diva remembers. "The thing about me is I hate knitting scarves. I hate it. They're the worst. . . . Even though [Emilio's] all in

"I grew up in a family where basically what you do is you learn all the rules so you can bend them and break them. You learn how to do things, but then you find a way of doing it that makes sense to you."

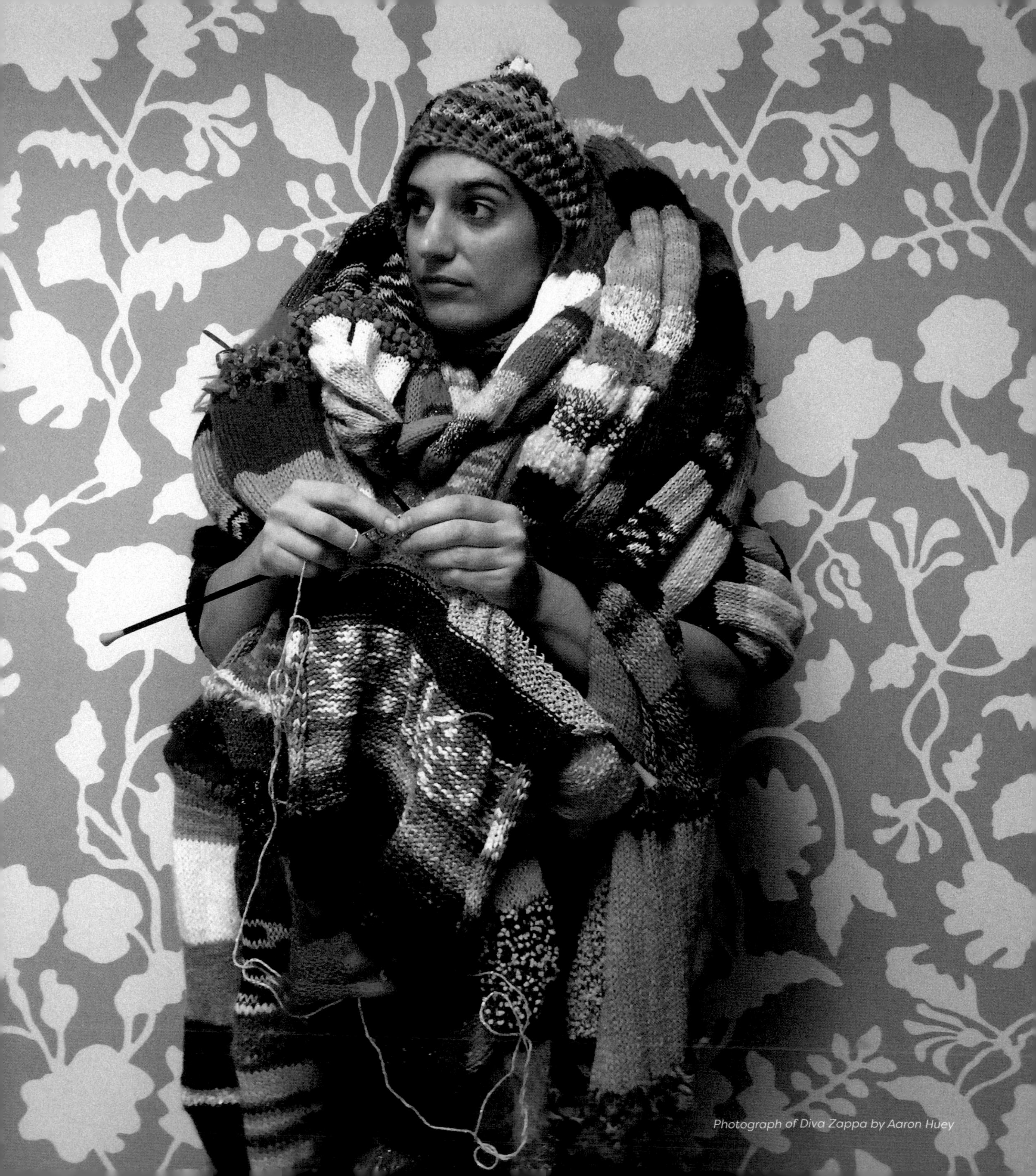

Photograph of Diva Zappa by Aaron Huey

one direction, though, he's still so many other things. He's in stockinette stitch and using the same set of needles, but in different materials, different yarns, different colors, different moods, different tones."

At ten years old, Emilio is still an infant as far as Diva's concerned. She says, "He's still a baby because he doesn't let me work on him every day. He's like, 'I'm not inspired, go away,' or he's on display in an art exhibit and I don't get to visit him every day."

The experience of Emilio is interactive. There's a symbiotic relationship between Diva the human and Emilio as a creative object. He's a living journal, according to Zappa, laying out the roadmap of her life.

"I've been working on it for so long and so much has happened in this time. You can see and feel different emotional pockets of my life and times when it was super happy and hilarious, and times when it was really in the thick of things. It's impressive when he's out and on display for people to see, and also just to experience this is what time passing actually looks like." Diva continues, "Every stitch is an example of the desire to know if what you're doing daily means something and adds up. That's what Emilio is. Proof. He's interactive and inspiring in that way." This living collection of stitches is like a physical manifestation of energy and, for Diva, her choices. Working on him has taught her about interaction, communication, and how there's meaning in everything one does. She posits, "Every stitch, it's energy, it's movement, it's time passing. It stacks on itself and it becomes something else." He's a marathon meditation for her.

When Diva gets to a mile, whenever that may be in the far future (at the time of this writing the scarf measures about four hundred feet), she has every intention of seeing what he wants to do next. This could be unraveling. It could be continuing on to a lengthier goal. It could mean cutting him up and having bits of him to share so everyone gets to have an experience. Emilio may not have a linear beginning and end, like a regular scarf would. His path may lead to fading into a different part of the overall journey. Diva believes that's what life is. "You have choices every day how you want to interact with things, how you want to be seen, how you want to feel, and that's the story that you get to experience with Emilio."

SIEDAH GARRETT

I chatted with Siedah Garrett via Skype from her home studio in L.A. about what inspires her to knit, sing, and live out loud.

VH: *Siedah, you're the epitome of creativity, because you're a writer, you're a singer, you're a performer, and you're a knitter and crocheter. Your skills blow me away. Let's go back. During your childhood as you're moving around, what was the origin of your creativity? Were you writing from the beginning? Were you crocheting from the beginning? How were you expressing yourself creatively in your youngest years?*

SG: I didn't know what I was doing, but I was singing, and my mother was always a guest in somebody's church. She would drag me along and prop me up onstage. I'd sing for the people. Also, when I was in one of the elementary schools, there was girl named Jackie and I just loved her. She was just a girly girl and I was so not. But I was attracted to her because she would sit and knit during recess and lunch. I didn't know how to knit and really wanted to learn, but I didn't have the tools. What I did was, I went home and took apart two metal hangers, and the long rod on the bottom where you fold your pants over, I bent the hangers until they broke so I had two hanger rods that I would try and knit with. I took apart an acrylic sweater, rolled it into a ball, and started to knit. My mother was so embarrassed that I was knitting with pieces of hanger and a sweater that I had taken apart that she actually bought me a pair of knitting needles and a ball of yarn. That's what started it.

SIEDAH GARRETT is an Oscar-nominated and Grammy-winning songwriter with credits under her belt like "Man in the Mirror" (yeah, that one, made iconic by Michael Jackson) and Jennifer Hudson's breakout song from the movie *Dreamgirls*, "Love You I Do." She also happens to be one helluva knitting and crochet designer.

VH: *That's pretty ingenious. Have you approached all aspects of your life with that kind of ingenuity? With that kind of moxie?*

SG: I don't know. I guess when you don't have, you make do. I just thought that would be a great thing.

VH: *You're singing wherever your mother props you up, you're knitting at that point. Had you started crocheting?*

SG: I didn't learn to crochet until there was a crossing guard who watched the children in the schoolyard, and she would sit and crochet, but she had elephantiasis, so she didn't walk around. She would just sit on a bench, crochet, and she would blow her whistle when she saw somebody running, or hitting, or whatever they were doing. Then, she'd go back to her crocheting. I would sit and watch her, so she just sort of took me under her wing and taught me to crochet. I thank her every day, 'cause she opened up a whole new world for me. For me, it was a lot easier than knitting. I could just work things out in my head without a pattern with crocheting that I couldn't do at that young age when I was knitting.

VH: *Because crochet is more sculptural?*

SG: Yes, absolutely. You don't really need a pattern to make something. If you know the stitches, you can make any kind of shape you want, not necessarily so with knitting. Knitting is more math.

VH: *So, when you're not stitching something, your mom has you singing for the people. Clearly, eventually that paid off.*

SG: When I was fifteen, my mother was hanging someone's wallpaper, an R&B artist named D.J. Rogers. She hung his wallpaper, and while she was hanging in his house she says, "You know, my daughter can sing." He was like, "Yeah, your daughter, my plumber's daughter," he was just saying whatever, but my mother was very persistent. He said, "All right. Bring her over and I'm telling you, if it's not happening, I don't want to hear about it anymore." So I went to his house, he sat me on the piano bench next to him. He played a riff on the piano and he said, "Sing this." I sang it and he was like, "Whoa. Okay." Then he said, "Sing this." Then he played a more complicated riff and I sang it, and he literally pushed me off the bench. The next thing I know, I'm in a recording session with these famous background singers. An audition for Quincy Jones, writing "Man in the Mirror" for Michael Jackson, touring with some of the biggest stars out there, the rest is history!

VH: *Incredible. Seeing the creativity you attract, it seems like you infuse the essence of living your spirit and loving your work into all that you do.*

SG: Vickie, seeing is believing. You are right on the money. I can't not be creative. I have to be doing something. I never sit idle and watch TV. When I'm in the dentist's office waiting to get my teeth cleaned, I'm knitting, or I'm crocheting, I'm always doing something. I also paint and sculpt as well, but I don't have as much fun doing that as I do working with the yarn.

VH: *Speaking of sitting idly, every musician I've known has talked about all of the downtime involved in touring. While you were touring with Michael Jackson, or Madonna, or whomever, did you fill that time with craft?*

SG: Oh my God, yes. I've knitted on planes, trains, on buses. I have knitted all over the world in every circumstance, in every situation you could find yourself in, where I was sitting idle waiting on a plane, or waiting on a bus, or waiting in line, I would just be knitting or crocheting.

VH: *Does coming up with your own inspired knitted piece or crochet piece fill the same creative space as writing a song? Does it feel different?*

SG: It's different. It's completely different. It's like, do you like skating or do you like riding your bike? I like them both, but they're both different. I enjoy every aspect of every bit of the creative process. I really, really do. I try to get it into my life at every opportunity.

VH: *I'm floored by some of the knit and crochet pieces you've designed. They're so imaginative, layered, and interesting. When you spoke at Vogue Knitting LIVE a few years back, you told many great stories about your music life, but also about some of the knit and crochet pieces you've created for people. Would you please share your story about Madonna and the bustier?*

SG: Yes. We were rehearsing before we went on the summer tour, the Reinvention Tour. There was a lot of downtime, and when Madonna was performing a number, if you weren't in the number, you had to sit in the audience in case she wanted to go over the number you were in. We're in an empty theater, sitting on benches, and I'm knitting this bustier inspired by the girlfriend of somebody on the tour. She came on the elevator wearing this piece that cost several hundred dollars, and I thought, *Hmmm. I could make that.* So I did. It was a simple, simple thing. A long rectangle of stockinette that I then closed, and put a zipper, and then attached it to a bra. Part of the bra would hang over the bustier so it would look like you have on a bustier that's slightly falling down. Madonna loved it, so I said, "I'll make you one." I said, "What color would you like it to be?" She said, "Oh, I think I would like a dusty rose," so I made it for her.

VH: *I've seen some of your bag designs that remind me of Chanel. What's the story behind those?*

SG: I got into making purses when I was walking down the street in Venice on Abbot Kinney in L.A., and I walked into this shop. They had crocheted bags that gave me the idea of crocheting with sequins. I started crocheting with them, and that put such an intricate detail on every bag. I went crazy. I gave one to my girlfriend, who went to some event where Angela Bassett tapped her on the shoulder and said, "Oh my God. That's a great bag! Where did you get it?" So I made Angela Bassett a few bags. She has a few of my bags, Madonna has my vest. I enjoy knowing that in some very famous people's closets hang some of my most intricate and delightful pieces.

ELISABETH WARD

Elisabeth is a British writer, content marketer, knitter, crocheter, and YouTuber.

KNITTING AND CROCHETING BEYOND MY DISABILITY

On my website I chronicle my life as a congenital amputee navigating an average-abled world. I started my blog to share some of my experiences growing up with a disability. It's my hope that its existence might help others like me who have struggled to come to terms with what it means to be different, and the consequences of it.

As a kid, I was bullied. Not directly for my disability, but really, for the way I was handling it. I felt very lost, very alone. I couldn't see who I was past what I thought everyone else saw: my disability. I was scared about what the future held for me and I could only see the negative. Then, there wasn't the internet to offer a window into a broader network.

It was only at university that my perspective began to change. Then when I got my first permanent job, my confidence grew and I became more centered. The people I worked with showed me I had value, and I worked hard to prove I could be just as good as anyone else.

I slowly realized how strong I am. Living one-handed has driven me to persevere until I can do something fully. When you're disabled, you always have to find ways around a barrier and keep going until you can do it. Otherwise you'll never do anything without having to ask for help all the time. I still ask for help, but I'll try to go it alone first . . . and that requires determination.

Crafting came to me because a roommate at university started knitting. I watched her start with a ball of yarn and end up with the cutest strawberry baby hat! I was so jealous. I wanted to be able to knit too, but I just couldn't see how. I resigned myself to the fact that I would never be able to knit. Later, when I was working full time, I stumbled into a home store that sold really cheap knitting needles and yarn. I bought them on impulse, thinking I'd work out the "how" later. A couple of YouTube videos later and I was addicted.

I started crocheting a few months later after a colleague made a comment that he thought I'd have found it easier. I'd never heard of crocheting and of course instantly looked into this mysterious craft. I found it much harder to start with; I couldn't use the standard hooks and needed versions with a handle. I was lucky that the strap I use to hold a knife for meals perfectly fit the hook, though. It gave me more movement and stability, so it was much easier and I became faster.

At this point I would've said crochet was easier because I was knitting with the yarn wrapped around my amputee arm, which was quite frustrating, as I couldn't regulate the flow of yarn. Because I'd learned how to control yarn in my left hand for crochet, though, I was then able to transfer that skill over to knitting.

It was a bit fiddly to start with, working out how I was going to hold the yarn in place on the right side of the needle when I was holding it taut with the left hand, but with a bit of perseverance I got it.

There were definitely tears of frustration during the learning process for both crafts but now I wouldn't say one is harder than the other, at least not from a physical perspective. Crochet is perhaps more tiring, both for my hand/arm and my brain!

I love the fact that you start with yarn, essentially a long bit of string, and create something beautiful and often useful. And you made it. Your hard work went into creating something from basically nothing. It's such a wonderful sense of achievement and pride. For me it's doubly so because I worked really hard to find ways I could do it without the second hand, all the while learning two new crafts from scratch.

At the beginning, when I was trying to teach myself online, I searched for one-handed knitting and crochet tutorials. The only videos that came up, though, were two-handed people doing it "one-handed." They weren't any showing practical solutions for how to stitch when you had less range of motion (especially crochet).

Once I mastered stitching with one hand for myself, I wanted to share how I'd done it just in case there were others like me who wanted to learn but didn't think they could. It can feel really frustrating, and even isolating, when there's a barrier in front of something you want to do and you're not sure how to get around it. I wanted to help people to push that barrier down.

They might need to use a slightly different method or find extra tools, but at least I've shown how to get started and that it can be done. It seems that the videos have actually succeeded in doing that. I've had a few really kind messages, often from amputees and those who've had strokes, who've used my videos to help them find success with their knitting and crochet. It makes me so happy to know that I'm making a difference.

I hope that through my website and videos that I'm sending a clear message: Keep going. Keep trying until you can do it. There were so many times when I was not getting anywhere and I wanted to give up. I was cursing the world for my difference and saying, "This is physically impossible, why am I even trying? I can't do this!" But I kept going. I looked for alternative tools, like the crochet hooks with thick soft handles, or metal knitting needles that made it easier to slide the yarn over. I looked for things in my house that I could use to help me, such as using the extra strap I was sent with my iPhone running armband, which could strap the crochet hook to my arm. There may not be something designed for your exact purpose, but there will be other things you can repurpose to meet this need.

Here are some tips to get you started: When knitting, find a position that feels comfortable for the nonworking needle. I find under my arm most comfortable, but you can position it between your legs if that's easier. If you have no use of one side, a clamp of some kind will work—anything that will hold the needle still.

For crochet, the best tool I've found is something that will strap the hook to your arm. This gives you more flexibility, stability, and range of motion than holding the hook against a surface with your hand. If you can't use your amputee arm or don't have movement on that side, again possibly hold the hook between your legs or a clamp. You don't need the hook to move, you can still crochet just using your working hand, so anything you can find that will hold the hook still is ideal.

The bottom line: Don't be afraid to get a bit creative about finding tools that work for you and be prepared for some setbacks along the way. Persevere, though, because it pays off. It has for me. And who knows, maybe next I'll tackle cross-stitch!

THE KNIT HIVE

KNIT HIVE /NIT HĪV/

(noun) A nod to the knitting bees of old and the modern "hive mind" mentality that refers to the gathering of stitchers, either physically or virtually, for the purpose of supporting and sharing a common passion for knitting, crochet, charts, and creativity.

HOW TO START A KNIT HIVE

Reading this book? Guess what: You're already a part of our Knit Hive (a term I originally came up with during the production of my series *The Knit Show*). So happy to have you!

Want to start your own? Do it! Community is a great gift to creativity and humanity. Go, you! Here are a few tips for getting one started.

Put it on the calendar.
Putting communal creative time on the calendar is a great way to make sure it happens. Pick a date for folks to meet up a home, bar, or community center. Psst . . . if you keep the date and time consistent, your hive is more likely to grow over time!

Stay local.
Local knitting shops are a great place to meet up with fellow Knit Hivesters. Ask the store owner if there's an evening that would work to hold a regular meet-up. I'd be willing to bet they'd not only be thrilled to host, but would also help spread the word through signs and e-newsletter mentions!

Be a lady or lad who lunches.
Lunchtime at the workplace is a great opportunity to fit in a few stitches while hanging with coworkers. Send out an email or post on an office board that you're looking for fellow crafters to snack and stitch with during breaks. Oh, and if you get any side eye from the higher-ups, just tell them you're team building!

Get social.
Can't get out to regular physical Knit Hive meetups? No problem—that's why we have the internet! Start a virtual group on Facebook, Ravelry, or another platform of your choice. It's free and easy, and offers an accessible way to touch base and stitch along with community members worldwide.

Sip and stitch.
Wine bars and pubs can be a fun place to do a crafty meet-up. Sip on your favorite spirits while you stitch with friends and strangers alike. Guess what? Knitting can be a great social lubricant—it gives purpose to striking up convo. Oh, and I suppose, the bevies couldn't hurt either!

THE
INTENTION

Knitting, or however we choose to express ourselves creatively, carries over to all aspects of life. It enriches, it empowers, it opens us up. This section focuses on the physical, mental, and spiritual well-being of you, dear stitcher.

KNITTING & THE BODY

YOGA FOR KNITTERS, WITH ALICIA MONTOYA

UNLOCK THE HEART

Shoulder opener; upper back and wrist stretch.

1. Sit in a comfortable cross-legged position. Sit up tall.

2. Bring your hands into fists at your heart center. Thumbs are on top; the fists are not touching; arms are parallel to the floor. Breathe deeply into the chest and exhale; notice your shoulder blades and draw them down.

3. Start to pull your arms away from each other slowly, reaching your fists out to opposite sides as if you're opening the doors of a heavy gate. Simultaneously continue to draw your shoulder blades down. Take a deep inhale, then an exhale, drawing your shoulders down another inch so that they kiss, moving them away from your ears, drawing your ribs down.

4. Inhale; extend your fists a little farther. Exhale, and once your arms are fully extended out to your sides, leading with your thumbs, tip them down like you're pouring two (hot and full) teapots out to the sides. Continue drawing your shoulder blades down. Take a deep inhale, pause, and exhale slowly.

5. Lift your thumbs back to neutral; spread your fingers out wide. Keeping your arms in place, reach your fingers back a little farther. Take an even deeper inhale. Exhale fully.

6. Last, draw your arms in and around yourself in an embrace.

ALICIA MONTOYA is a yoga instructor, homeschooler, and mother. She lives in Southern California with her husband and two children and their dog, Scotch. She teaches pre- and postnatal yoga throughout the South Bay area.

THREAD THE NEEDLE

Releases upper back tension. Stretches shoulders, arms, chest, and upper back.

1. Start on your hands and knees in a neutral position (wrists under your shoulders, hips above your knees, feet straight behind you, head and neck in line with your spine).

2. Inhale and lift your right arm straight up toward the ceiling.

3. Exhale, releasing the right arm and threading it under your left armpit. You will land on your right shoulder and the right side of your face.

   Notice your hips; they should remain over your knees.

4. Repeat for opposite side.

WRIST RELEASE

Stretch for weary wrists.

1. From a standing position, slowly hinge forward, lengthening as you go.

2. Place your hands under your feet with your toes at the wrist crease. Lean into the stretch as appropriate, and wiggle your toes to massage your wrists.

3. Bend your knees to modify for what feels right for you.

PYRAMID POSE

1. Stand with your arms at your sides, feet grounded into the earth, hip-width distance apart, shoulders rolling down away from the ears.

2. Take your hands to your hips and take the left foot back approximately 3 feet (hip-width distance). Rotate the left foot at a 75-to-80-degree angle; the hips are square. Anchor the right hip back and left hip forward.

3. Bring your arms back behind you and clasp opposite hands to opposite elbows. (Use a strap/belt if needed.) Take in a deep inhale and exhale as you broaden your shoulders and collarbones. Rooting your left heel into the earth, deeply inhale. Exhale and pull the belly in, lower the ribs in. Inhale, lengthening your chest, slightly arch the chest and lift the head up. Lift the sternum to the sky. The tailbone is reaching down.

4. Center your torso over your front thigh and hinge down from the hips halfway, elongating through the spine. Soften your shoulder blades down, spreading the collarbones very wide. Stay connected with the core; the fingers are holding the elbows (or strap/belt if needed), not grasping too tightly.

5. Continue to square your hips while your left ribs are reaching forward and the right hip continues to reach back.

   * Bend the front knee slightly if needed.

6. To release, anchor both feet into the earth, inhale, and rise, lifting from the core and sternum. Release your elbows down to your sides; lift your left foot to meet the right.

7. Continue on the other side.

EXERCISES FOR CORE STRENGTH & STABILITY, WITH FITNESS TRAINER BRITNY FOWLER

When it comes to knitting, crocheting, or really any activity for which you have forward posture, or over-repetitive movement, you've got to think about combating the effects of that so you can continue doing what you love pain-free, or at least eliminating or diminishing some of that pain. That comes with core strength; the torso has everything to do with it. "Core" is collarbone to mid-thigh, not just abs but your glutes and your shoulder blades as well. All of these things work together to set you up for the best breathing capabilities, for the best posture, and to help you feel better, move better, and therefore, keep doing what you really love. Here are three exercises to help keep you stitching!

BRITNY FOWLER is an Austin, Texas–based personal trainer and presenter, providing training and education for several education companies, including Trigger Point, TRX, Hyperwear, and Lifetime Fitness. She teaches group strength, cardio, cycle, and Pilates classes. Britny has appeared in YouTube's *The Knit Show*, encouraging physical health for stitchers, and the A&E series *Heavy* as a trainer to clients facing life-threatening health consequences as a result of their obesity.

Y TO W EXERCISE

1. Begin facedown to the ground; activate from the core by pulling your belly button in, away from the mat; activate your glutes (pretend you're pinching a penny with them). Eyes look straight down at the mat. Stretch arms out long like a swimmer into an I or Y formation.

2. With your shoulder blades pulled down in the back, float the arms back to a W formation.

3. Repeat by reaching back out into a Y, and pulling back down into a W. The key is to maintain core activation and shoulder-blade stability.

BRIDGE POSE

1. On your back, bend your knees, feet flat, arms by your sides. Think: space in the waist and space in the neck.

2. Push down into the ground with your feet. Core and glutes are now activated. Driving from the hips, press them toward the sky. Here you can feel that posterior side working, which is really good, beneficial for opening up so we can access the abs. So we have good lengths, we feel this through the core, through the abs, through the glutes.

3. Roll down bone by bone, so there's articulation, all the way through the tailbone.

PLANK & YARN EXERCISE

For this exercise, you'll need a ball or hank of yarn. Seriously.

1. With feet hip distance apart, hands (or elbows*) under shoulders, and core and glutes engaged, think "head-to-heel, beam of steel." Press up into a strong plank position.

2. From here, your goal is to rotate the yarn with one hand; set down the yarn. Repeat with other hand. The goal is minimum movement (i.e., rotating and shifting through the hips), so that if someone were to see you from behind, they wouldn't know you were lifting your hands. Stay engaged in your shoulders, glutes, legs, and core, and you'll see the most success!

 * *If you have wrist issues, modify this exercise by working from your forearms instead of your wrists (see photo 3)!*

DIETARY RECOMMENDATIONS FOR HEALTHY BONES, JOINTS & MUSCLES, BY DR. MICHELLE LANE

Many people do not eat enough of the nutrients that promote bone and joint health. The nutrients calcium and vitamin D are crucial for bone health. Omega-3 polyunsaturated fatty acids may help joints stay free of pain and improve brain function.

How these nutrients work:

CALCIUM is a crucial component of bone. An adequate intake of calcium through your midtwenties increases your peak bone mineral density (BMD, assessed in osteoporosis screenings). Once you are past your midtwenties your BMD will start to decrease. If your BMD decreases too much, osteoporosis may result. To preserve as much bone as possible and avoid osteoporosis, adult women before age fifty (and men aged nineteen to seventy) should eat foods containing 1,000 mg of calcium each day. Women fifty-one and over (and men seventy-one and over) should consume 1,200 mg per day. In addition to eating enough calcium, daily weight-bearing exercise and enough vitamin D are crucial to maintaining bone health. Weight-bearing exercises include weight training, walking, hiking, and jogging. Weight-bearing exercises help bones remain healthy by causing your bones to constantly rebuild themselves, increasing muscle tone, and improving coordination, all of which prevent the falls that can lead to fractures.

VITAMIN D allows calcium to be absorbed by your intestines. It also allows your bones to rebuild themselves, fixing daily wear and tear. Depending on where you live, your skin can make your own vitamin D from the UVB rays in sunlight. The closer you live to either pole, the less likely it is that your skin can make enough, though, particularly in the winter when the days are shorter. Clothing, darker skin, and

MICHELLE A. LANE, PHD, is a crocheter and an associate professor in the Nutrition and Foods Program at Texas State University. She teaches genetics and biochemistry and is the director of the graduate program in human nutrition. Her research aims to determine how the maternal diet can prevent postpartum depression as well as how omega-3 poly-unsaturated fatty acids decrease colorectal cancer metastasis. Dr. Lane earned her BS in animal science at Cornell University and her PhD in nutrition at Rutgers University. Her postdoctoral work in pharmacology was conducted at the Weill Medical College of Cornell University.

sunscreen prevent your skin from making vitamin D. Air pollution, cloud cover, and your age also affect your skin's ability to make it. It doesn't take much time for your skin to make enough vitamin D to meet your needs. If you live below 33 degrees latitude, on a sunny summer day, around the middle of the day, you need only five to thirty minutes of sun exposure, twice a week, to your face, arms, or back (without sunscreen). Despite our ability to make our own vitamin D, many people are deficient in this nutrient. In this case, vitamin D–rich foods can meet our needs. Individuals ages nineteen to sixty-nine should aim to consume 600 IU (international units) of vitamin D per day. People seventy and over should eat 800 IU each day.

OMEGA-3 POLYUNSATURATED FATTY ACIDS appear to decrease inflammation and may lessen pain. They may also increase mental acuity and decrease depression. The omega-3 polyunsaturated fatty acids found in our diet include alpha-linolenic acid (ALA), eicosapentaenoic acid (EPA), and docosahexaenoic acid (DHA). ALA is found in plants and can be converted to EPA by our bodies, but this process is very inefficient. EPA and DHA, found in fish oils, are the biologically active omega-3 polyunsaturated fatty acids. The National Institutes of Health recommend that adult, nonpregnant women and men consume 1.1 and 1.6 g of ALA, respectively, each day. There are no dietary guidelines for EPA and DHA in the United States, but the European Food Safety Authority recommends that adults consume 250 mg (0.25 g) per day of EPA and DHA, based on the ability of these nutrients to decrease heart disease.

Dietary sources of these nutrients:

Research shows that the nutrients listed above work best when eaten as a part of a food, rather than taken as a pill. For example, calcium supplements do not improve bone health but dairy products do. Similarly, pills containing EPA and DHA do not decrease depression, but having higher levels of these fats in your diet correlates with lower rates of depression in population-based studies. Also, ingesting more than what you need of a nutrient can result in toxicity. When eaten as part of food, it is almost impossible to ingest toxic levels of the nutrients listed below:

Calcium is highest in low-fat dairy products such as milk, cheese, and yogurt. Plant-based sources of calcium include tofu (if prepared with calcium sulfate), white beans, Chinese cabbage, kale, and figs.

Vitamin D is highest in fish such as salmon, swordfish, and trout. Other than fish, few foods contain vitamin D. Mushrooms exposed to UV light have some vitamin D. Additional foods are fortified with vitamin D, including low-fat milk, orange juice, and some cereals.

Omega-3 polyunsaturated fatty acids are found in their bioactive forms, EPA and DHA, at high levels in fatty fish such as mackerel, salmon, tuna, herring, sardines, and anchovies. Eggs and milk can contain EPA and DHA if these fats are added after processing or fed to chickens or cattle, respectively. Plants contain ALA. Plant sources of ALA include flaxseed (and oil), chia seeds, walnuts, soybean, and canola oil.

Sources of information related to nutrition:

Your best source for information regarding nutrition is a registered dietitian nutritionist. Good websites for nutrition-related information should end with ".org" or ".gov." The ".com" ending indicates that website is trying to sell you something. Reliable sources for nutrition information include:

The American Institute for Cancer Research:
AICR.org

The United States Department of Agriculture:
health.gov/dietaryguidelines

The National Institutes of Health:
www.nhlbi.nih.gov/health/educational/wecan/
tools-resources/nutrition.htm

The Center for Science in the Public Interest:
cspinet.org

THE NEUROSCIENCE OF CREATIVITY & MINDFULNESS AND KNITTING, BY CHELSEA DEKRYUFF, MA, LPC

CHELSEA DEKRYUFF is a knitter, psychotherapist, life coach, and spiritual director in private practice in Austin, Texas.

NEUROSCIENCE OF CREATIVITY

As a psychotherapist who specializes in applied neuroscience and mindfulness, one of my areas of interest is helping artists better access their creativity. If you're a knitter or crocheter and you want a little bit more creativity in your work, if you feel you've reached a plateau, or if it's just kind of stopped being fun, let me give you a few ideas about how you might think about your brain differently to better help you access that creativity. To begin, let's talk about your brain and where creativity comes from.

When we think about the brain, we have your right hemisphere and your left hemisphere. The right side of your brain is generally where you have music, an appreciation of beauty, art, spirituality, sexuality, memory. It's where all of these kinds of mysterious and more abstract parts of you exist.

The left side of your brain is where we register linear time, language, deadlines, categories, procedures, and getting things just right. It's also where we have perfectionism. Sometimes when people are engaged in creative acts, they'll get so caught up in having it be just perfect that they're not even in the part of the brain where the good ideas are coming from.

Consider this: Next time you're working on a project and perhaps your gauge is off or the pattern just isn't quite right, if you can cut yourself a little slack and have a little bit more fun and just play with it, and not be so caught up in getting it perfect, then you'll likely notice better ideas presenting themselves and your whole entire experience becoming more enjoyable.

"SOMETIMES WHEN PEOPLE ARE ENGAGED IN CREATIVE ACTS, THEY'LL GET SO CAUGHT UP IN HAVING IT BE JUST PERFECT, THAT THEY'RE NOT EVEN IN THE PART OF THE BRAIN WHERE THE GOOD IDEAS ARE COMING FROM."

THE MINDFULNESS OF KNITTING & CROCHET

Mindfulness is a present-moment awareness of your experience, as it arises, without judgment. This process relates easily to needlework. For example, as you're knitting one, purling two, you're paying attention to the pattern that you're using, and hopefully not judging each moment as good or bad, right or wrong, just paying attention to that moment.

The benefits of mindfulness, and being in that state, are many. There's lots of neuroscience that's been done on what happens to the brain when you're in this present moment. For one thing, the part of your brain, your corpus callosum, that connects your right and left hemispheres gets thicker and denser, so you're able to go back and forth between both sides of your brain more readily.

The fibers in your prefrontal cortex, which is long-term consequences, strategy, problem solving, that's the part of you that allows you to play chess better than your cat. It's also the part of your brain that allows for emotional regulation, and empathy, your ability to connect with other people.

All of those parts of your brain grow, so the act of being mindful is something that changes the shape of your brain. We usually think of our brain as something static, and it's not. Just like you can increase the size of your biceps by curling a dumbbell, the act of bringing your attention from the past or future, back to the present moment, actually changes the structure and shape of your brain, and allows you to calm down and reason better.

With knitting or crocheting, I recommend choosing a pattern that's just challenging enough to keep you engaged, but not so challenging as to cause frustration. By doing this, and if you can use your stitching as a way to focus yourself in that moment, then you're going to do a lot for your brain!

SPINNING, KNITTING & JUDAISM, WITH RABBI SUSAN ELKODSI

The Torah teaches that we are God's partners, on earth, in creating a better world. The idea that God spoke and the world came into being certainly goes along with any type of crafting, because in a sense, we're creating a world, an entity.

Another connection between Judaism and crafts is that when the Israelites are in the wilderness and God commands that they build the sanctuary that will go with them, there are all kinds of references to people who are what in Hebrew is called *chochmat lev*, wise at heart and skilled. The women in particular are responsible for the textiles. There's a verse that talks about them spinning the hair right off the goat. The exercise and meditation to follow are in the spirit of those women.

KNITTING *SEFER YETZIRAH*, THE BOOK OF CREATION—AN EXERCISE

Sefer Yetzirah, the Book of Creation, is a guide to the cosmology and cosmogony of creation. We learn in *Bereshit* (Genesis) that at first, the universe was *tohu vavohu*—"unformed and void," and that God created the heavens and the earth, the water and the land, vegetation and animals, and, ultimately, humanity.

Sefer Yetzirah wants to understand what structures God created as a foundation of our material universe, and one way to participate in this process is through creating a concrete object. In this case, it's a knitted item that will help someone to learn about and better understand Chapter 3 in the Book of Creation.

RABBI SUSAN ELKODSI is the spiritual leader of the Malverne (New York) Jewish Center and became a rabbi later in life, in 2015, receiving ordination from the Academy for Jewish Religion. Before becoming a rabbi, Susan worked in the advertising field and, with her husband, David, raised two terrific kids, Phillip and Jacqueline, who unfortunately haven't picked up on their mother's passion for fiber arts.

"A LARGE PART OF THE KNITTING PROCESS COMES IN MINDFULLY CHOOSING THE YARNS FOR THE PROJECT, AND HOPEFULLY NOT OVERTHINKING."

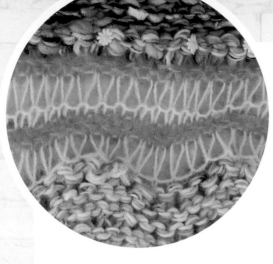

ART PIECE EXER-CISE: KNITTING *SEFER YETZIRAH*, THE BOOK OF CREATION

MATERIALS

6 yarns, in varying weights and three different color families

Colors A & B will be *Shin*, C & D will be *Aleph*, and E & F will be *Mem*

Large knitting needles (US 17 or above)

DIRECTIONS

Holding 6 strands together, CO 32 sts.

Rows 1–2: Using all 6 strands, knit.

This is the beginning of the transformation from chaos to order, and it represents the Divine breath that will bring forth the elements.

Rows 3–12: With colors A and B held together (OR alternating separately over the course of these 10 rows), knit.

From the Divine breath comes fire.

Rows 13–14: Using A, B, C, and D held together, knit.

The addition of C and D represents air, *Aleph*. Here is where *Aleph* provides synthesis between the other two.

Cut colors A and B (*Shin*).

This represents the light and elusiveness of air, as the piece will begin to take on a more open look and feel.

Rows 15–16: With C, knit.

Row 17: With D, k each st, wrapping the yarn around the needle TWICE for each st.

Row 18: Knit, dropping extra wraps.

Rows 19–30: Rep Rows 15–18.

Join colors E and F (*Mem*).

Rows 31, 32, and 34: With C, D, E, and F held together, knit.

Rows 33: K1, *[k2tog] twice, [yo, k1] four times, k2tog; rep from * to last st, k1.

This represents where the air meets and becomes integrated with the water. The "wave lace" pattern of the rows denotes water.

Cut C and D; cont. with E and F.

Rows 35–46: Rep Rows 31–34.

BO.

FINISHING

Weave in ends.

Using desired color combination(s), make and add fringe to bottom of piece. This represents the Divine breath flowing downward through the elements.

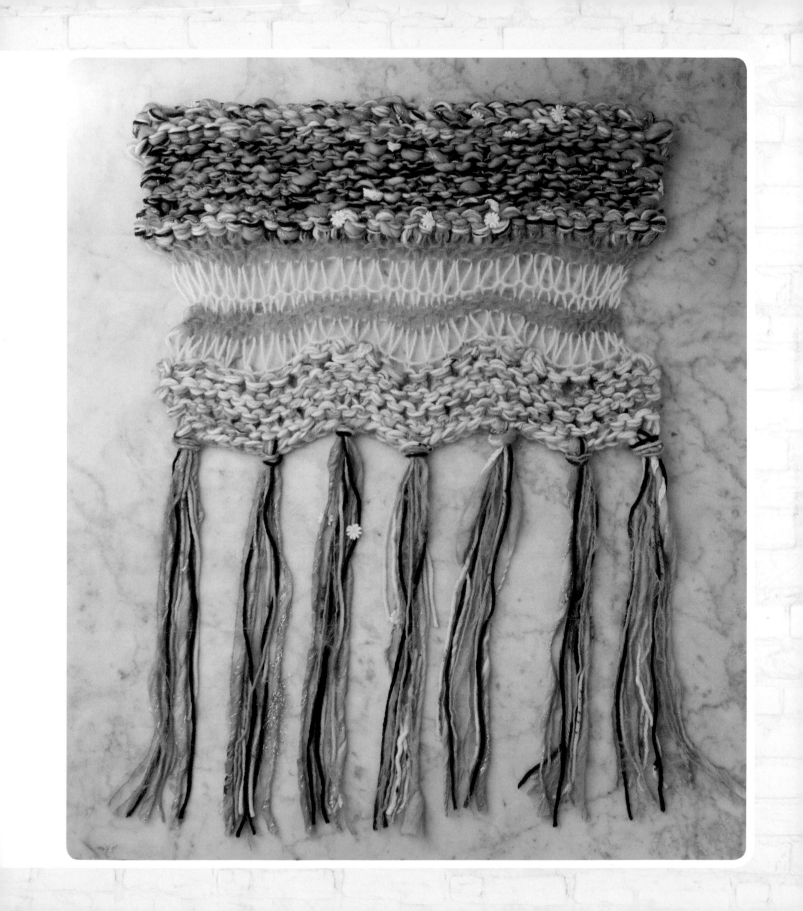

A MEDITATION FOR PERSONAL CREATION

Genesis (*Bereshit* in Hebrew) teaches us that humans are created *b'tzelem elo-him*, in the Divine image. In Judaism, we believe that God has no physical form, so this can't mean that we physically resemble God. What it does mean is that we are to emulate God, and to walk in God's ways—performing acts of charity and loving kindness and being God's partners in creating a better world.

In Exodus, when the construction of the sanctuary in the wilderness and its furnishings are about to begin, jobs are given to the Israelites. Those who are *chochmat lev*—wise of heart—fashion a variety of artifacts, including curtains and other textiles and even extending to spinning goat hair right off the goat!

When we knit, we create something special; whether it's for ourselves, a special gift, or for a donation. Knitting gives us an opportunity to slow down and to be mindful, or to keep our hands busy, allowing our brains to relax.

"As I sit down to knit this (item, swatch, etc.) may God bless my hands and my mind. May my mind be calm and focused and may the one for whom this is intended feel the blessing and peace I feel while I'm knitting it."

The three elements—air, fire, and water—emanate from the Divine breath that came out of the chaos to breathe life into and create the world. The first *Mishnah* (teaching) of *Sefer Yetzirah* says: "There are 32 wondrous paths of wisdom," and teaches us that God only needs 32 cosmic "action items" in order to create the universe.

The focus of Chapter 3 shifts to three "mother" letters, א-מ-ש, *Aleph*, *Mem,* and *Shin*, which represent a move toward balance. *Mem* is thesis, *Shin* is antithesis, and *Aleph* is synthesis. These three mother letters are both male and female, and present themselves in time, space, and the body/soul.

In the world or physical realm, *Shin* represents fire, *Aleph* represents air, and *Mem* represents water. While later mysticism (Kabbalah) assigns colors to the various elements, *Sefer Yetzirah* does not. For this project, choose two color families each to represent *Shin* (A, B), *Aleph* (C, D) and *Mem* (E, F).

The masculine and feminine aspects of the elements can be illustrated by using yarns of similar colors in different weights, by using two colors from the same family, by pairing a solid with a variegated yarn, or by using significantly different fibers. A large part of the knitting process comes in mindfully choosing the yarns for the project, and hopefully not overthinking. Needles should be large enough to accommodate the heaviest yarns, doubled. A larger-than-normal needle will give an open feel to the piece, and gauge is not critical. A note about the yarns for *Aleph*—it's nice if these yarns are very different in weight, and/or if one of them is a mohair type of yarn with a "halo."

KNITTING & THE CATHOLIC RITUAL OF EUCHARISTIC ADORATION

The Catholic religion is deeply entrenched in ritual. As a child I was always fascinated with the practice of using the rosary to guide prayer, each bead representing a repeat of prayer and intention. Although it has been decades since I've practiced myself, I still acknowledge the power of such traditions within the context of true faith.

My cousin Monty's wife, Mary Brown, is without a doubt the most devout and faithful Catholic I know. She also happens to be a knitter. It is from her that I learned about the practice of Eucharistic adoration, and how she uses her knitting, each stitch working much as one rosary bead might, to bring meditative focus to this sacred act. Furthermore, there is precedent for incorporating fiber works into divine worship. In the *Diary of St. Maria Faustina Kowalska* (3rd edition, Marian Press), which birthed the Divine Mercy Movement, St. Faustina wrote, "This morning after completing my spiritual exercises, I began at once to crochet. I sensed a stillness in my heart; I sensed that Jesus was resting in it. That deep and sweet consciousness of God's presence prompted me to say to the Lord, 'O Most Holy Trinity dwelling in my heart, I beg You: grant the grace of conversion to as many souls as the [number of] stitches that I will make today with this crochet hook."

WHILE PRAYING, IN
EITHER CONVERSATION
FORM OR REPETITIVE
PRAYERS, WORK STITCHES
AND ROWS IN RHYTHM
WITH YOUR THOUGHT.

A PRACTICE: EUCHARISTIC ADORATION FOR STITCHERS

During this time, usually an hour or so, a person or people sit quietly in church in front of a consecrated host (the presence of Jesus in the form of unleavened bread) that is displayed in a monstrance. While praying, in either conversation form or repetitive prayers, work stitches and rows in rhythm with your thought, using those stitches to represent a physical foundation of intention. The following is a repetition of prayers that might be used during this period of adoration.*

DIVINE MERCY CHAPLET

While working stitches in a row or round, recite the "Our Father," "Hail Mary," and "Apostle's Creed" prayers.

Begin new row or round. Pray,

"Eternal Father, I offer You the Body and Blood, Soul and Divinity of Your dearly beloved Son, Our Lord Jesus Christ, in atonement for our sins and those of the whole world."

Continue working stitches in row or round and say, *"For the sake of His sorrowful Passion have mercy on us and on the whole world."*

Finish off (row, round, or project) or find a stopping point and pray these words three times: *"Holy God, Holy Mighty One, Holy Immortal One, have mercy on us and on the whole world."*

* Sources: CatholicCompany.com and thedivinemercy.org.

NATIVE AMERICAN DYE STUFF HARVESTING RITUAL, WITH CANDICE ENGLISH

CANDICE ENGLISH is a mother, a dyer, the owner of The Farmer's Daughter Fibers, and a member of the Blackfeet tribe. Read more about Candice in her profile on page 31.

Gathering plants for craft and dyeing yarn is one of the most meaningful and substantial ways to connect with the earth. Harvesting in the wild warrants much research to make sure we are not taking rare species, are identifying plants correctly, and are being respectful of the spiritual power plants hold. We must give thanks to the Creator and to the plant itself for giving us the opportunity to use it for our creative intention, and to ensure that the power of the plant continues to live on spiritually. In the Blackfeet Tribe tradition, our elders have taught us to do this as follows:

Take a pinch of traditional tobacco for sprinkling, or sweetgrass, cedar, or sage for smudging.

Clear the mind to enable listening to the voices of wild;

Say a prayer for the plant about to be harvested, then sprinkle the tobacco on the ground (or commence smudging).

PRAYER FOR HARVESTING

"THANK YOU CREATOR FOR GIVING US THE POWER OF THESE PLANTS. WE GIVE YOU THIS OFFERING TO KEEP THE SPIRIT OF THESE PLANTS ALIVE IN OUR USES AND TO THANK YOU FOR YOUR GIFT."

YARN CRAFT & PAGANISM, WITH CHRISTIANE KNIGHT

TIPS:

Whether naturals, pastels, or brights, work with colors that speak to you!

Add incense, a candle, and/or a calming tea to your ritual to add gravitas and centering in the moment.

The fiber arts are so intertwined with nature—whether it be from animal or plant fibers, or vegetable and herb dyes—that it seems quite, well, natural to explore their connection with a religion rooted in the elements of the outdoors. Paganism, unlike its Wiccan sister, doesn't center around any deities but rather is a practice rooted in communing with all that is unmanufactured around us. Christiane uses her love of spinning and fiber as a physical focal point for meditation intended to ease the spirit and calm the mind.

SELF-ACTUALIZATION KNOTTED CORD RITUAL

We will be creating our cords by braiding and then knotting them a specific number of times, all while concentrating on an intention that we would like to see happen. I have used this primarily as a ritual-type process to set my focus on creating a specific outcome—like a directed meditation. Other uses are for manifesting, general meditation, to create a stim-toy for anxious moments or for general concentrating, when you need your hands to be busy so your mind can be calm. It is highly adaptable!

If you are a spinner, you can add a layer to this practice by spinning the yarn you will be using. Even better if you work with fiber prep or dyeing, as every layer of working with your materials creates a deeper and more meaningful connection. If you'd like to experience this but are not a fiber worker, you could consider using food coloring to dye some wool or wool-blend yarn to your specifications. Otherwise

CHRISTIANE KNIGHT has embraced a modern aesthetic of texture and color to convey energy, emotion, and movement. Self-taught, she espouses the idea of moving knitting, crochet, weaving, and other fiber arts from the dismissive label of "craft" to a full-fledged artistic form while keeping one foot in the modern world, the other in the realm of magical possibility.

you can just rummage through your stash and choose the yarns to work with that speak the strongest to you. Pick yarns that you will want to touch a lot and that aesthetically please you when combined. Each choice forges more of a connection with the process!

You will want the yarn strands you'll be working with to be either three or a multiple of three in number—each the same length and at least a yard long. I often measure from my elbow to fingertips three times to measure the length of yarn that I'll be working with, then use that yarn to measure the other strands.

You can combine your various yarn strands in any way you like (two of the same type and another of a different style or all from the same skein). Again, this is personal preference. I often will use two strands of a bulky and one of a novelty yarn like a bouclé, for the visual interest.

Divide your yarns into three sections; we will be making a long braid with them! I usually knot them together a couple of inches from the end—I like a decent fringe. This is again all to your preference.

Use a large safety pin to either fasten the knotted end to your pants leg or an upholstered piece of furniture. You just need something to hold it steady while you braid the yarns together. Another good way is to pin it to a cork board or, if your fringe is long enough, use that to tie the end to a kitchen chair.

"EVERY LAYER OF WORKING WITH YOUR MATERIALS CREATES A DEEPER AND MORE MEANINGFUL CONNECTION."

BRAIDING VARIATIONS

While you are braiding your yarns together, and every step forward in creating your cord, you should do your best to keep your mind on the intentions you want to achieve. I find that creating a complete atmosphere—in other words, a sort of sacred space—is really helpful. Candles, incense or smudging, and music that heightens the mood or helps you to be calm and focused can really add to the effect of your efforts. Think of it as a full ritual of self-care and actualization!

I usually braid my cord until five or six inches remain, then prepare to make a knot. This is where you will start to really focus on your intention, because we are going to make a series of knots in our cords, slowly infusing the cord with what we are focusing on. Each knot will "seal" that intention or thought into place, ritually, until we have nine knots in our cords.

I have a very specific way that I add the knots to my cord. The first knot is the one we began with, and the second will be the one that holds our cord together. Then I move to the middle of the cord and place a knot there.

x———————————————x———————————————x

From there, I add a knot between the first knot and the one in the middle, then between the middle knot and the ending knot.

1 x———————4———————3———————5———————x 2

The next knots go in between the ones we've created. I use this pattern, but if you mess up or choose to go straight down the cord, it doesn't matter. The important part is that you keep yourself focused on the result you're bringing into being with this cord and your energy.

1 x———6———4———8———3———9———5———7———x 2

You may find that the sections are different lengths. That doesn't matter, either. What does matter is the representation of your thoughts and actions combined! Sometimes cords that aren't perfect are much more aesthetically pleasing, too.

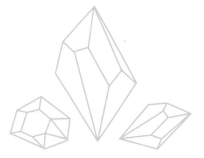

crystals

FOR
CREATIVITY—
QUICK
REFERENCE

MOOKAITE JASPER
Openness to new experiences

CITRINE
Imagination and abundance

LAPIS LAZULI
Inner power and manifestation

AMETHYST
Higher mind expansion, creativity enhancement

Now that you have your cord complete, you can put it into action! I usually trim the tassels on the ends of the cords. You can also tie the tassel ends together on one side and use that as a loop to fasten the cord to your wrist or ankle as a bracelet or anklet, if you like. I sometimes will tie mine on "permanently"—that is, until it wears out and falls off—when I'm working on manifesting something specific in my life. My theory is that when it finally falls off, my goal is either achieved or results are on the way!

If you use a natural material, you can wear these in the shower and throughout your day without much fuss. Again, do what seems natural to you; that's how this becomes your special meditation.

ANTI-ANXIETY CORD MEDITATION

Use each knot like a bead, and slowly run each "bead" through your fingers while thinking, "My anxiety is draining away, flowing harmlessly into the ground. A sense of calm flows into me. All will be well."

VISUALIZATION CORD MANTRA

Use each bead to mark the chant of a mantra or visualization. For example, "I am successful and supported by the Universe in all that I do."

Keep it positive, short, and very clear, and you'll find this a really productive activity! If you want to get a lot fancier, you can also include beads or charms on your cord. I kept this tutorial very simple specifically to make it accessible to everyone at any skill level. Please DO adapt it to your own needs and make this project your own!

KNITTER'S ASTROLOGY, BY KERRIANN GODWIN

KERRIANN GODWIN is a native Australian who now lives in the UK. She studied astrology in Sydney and London. When she was a child, her grandmother taught her to knit, and she has loved it ever since. For many years she helped to run the Museum of Witchcraft in Cornwall, which her partner, Graham King, owned before his recent retirement. It was here that she discovered the use of knitting in magic and prayer and how repetition and concentration focus the mind on the task at hand. She has published books for the museum and written for magazines on subjects as varied as motor homes, dogs, and astrology. Kerriann wrote the "Knitstrology" column for *Knit.1* magazine under the name Pearl Wise. She is now working on a book for middle-grade children that may involve a teeny bit of knitting.

AWESOME ARIES

Your fiery fingers can't wait to get cracking on yet another new knitting project, Aries. Your ever-ready enthusiasm and energy make it hard to keep focused for long, but you'll bathe in the glory of achievement when you actually cast off that final stitch. Keeping it small keeps it interesting.

Fire sign Aries rules heads and hats—suggested project: **a red hat** (for cute appeal).

TACTILE TAURUS

The caress of cashmere delights your sensitive digits, Taurus. Combine your flare and creativity with your practicality and you'll have no problem manifesting your tasteful ideas into stunning reality. Ensure you use needles that feel fabulous in your fingers—you deserve something special to complete your creations.

Earth sign Taurus rules the neck and throat—suggested project: an **emerald-green scarf** (to fling).

GENIAL GEMINI

Tap, tap, tap! "Which project will I work on today?" Stop fidgeting and get on with it, Gemini. Your active mind gives you so many great ideas it's hard to pick just one. Why not spread the word and share your creations? Join a knitting circle, design a pattern, or write a book (a knitting book, of course).

Air sign Gemini rules hands and arms—suggested project: a **lemon-yellow glove** (or two)

COMPASSIONATE CANCER

Caring, considerate, intuitive—to you knitting is not just a hobby, it's an expression of love and friendship. Each stitch is crafted with positive thoughts and affection. How pleasing to see the smiles on the faces of everyone who's lucky enough to receive one of your handcrafted gifts.

Water sign Cancer rules the home—suggested project: a **pearl-gray throw** (to spread the love).

LAVISH LEO

"Boring" just isn't in your knitting vocabulary, Leo. You're all about "solar glamour"—think Barbarella circa 1968. You rock glitzy gold metallic yarns, sunrise red hues—you're king (or queen) of the yarn jungle. You'll knit anything to attract attention so you can share your love of living with fun and passion.

Fire sign Leo rules the heart and spine—suggested project: a **golden swimsuit** (for va-va-voom).

VITAL VIRGO

Performing patterns of great intricacy is your idea of heaven, Virgo. "Bring me Fair Isle, intarsia, cables— I can do it all," you cry. Okay, okay, we get the picture. We know you're a perfectionist, we know you're a master of the craft, but everyone has to drop a stitch sometime. You *are* human after all—aren't you?

Earth sign Virgo rules herbs and hands—suggested project: **deluxe gardening gloves** (to dig daintily).

LUSCIOUS LIBRA

Decisions, decisions! Perfection is cool but wasting time is not; pick a pattern and run with it. There's no need to overthink it—with your inherent style and good taste, every choice will be the right one. Can't decide between two colors? Knit both—one for now and one for later.

Air sign Libra rules furniture and poetry—suggested project: a **pale rose cushion** (perfect for plumping).

SENSUOUS SCORPIO

What's Scorpio about? Life, death, and rebirth, that's what! Delve into the dark recesses of your closet, bring out an old sweater that's near death, and give it new life. Add sleeves, lose sleeves, make socks from sleeves, anything to get your creative juices flowing—and speaking of juices, the other thing about Scorpio . . .

Water sign Scorpio rules the sexual organs—suggested project: a **purple peignoir** (for midnight madness).

SEARCHING SAGITTARIUS

Stride out into the world with your knitting bag by your side, Sagittarius. Your fingers are ever ready for inspiration from your exotic travels to far-flung destinations. A poncho here, a balaclava there, a knitted something everywhere! Your thirst for new ideas is almost unquenchable—drink from the cup of life.

Fire sign Sagittarius rules explorers and foreign affairs—suggested project: a **patchwork travel blanket** (for toasty thighs).

COOL CAPRICORN

Step by step, stitch by stitch, you conquer each pattern with patience and efficiency, Capricorn. "Difficult, shmifficult," you cry. No one learned anything from knitting stuff the easy way. That multi-cabled mountaineering cape isn't going to knit itself—grab life by the horns and go for it.

Earth sign Capricorn rules knees and mountains—suggested project: a **triple-knit black sock** (times two).

AMAZING AQUARIUS

Eccentric and imaginative patterns spill from your multicolored knitting bag, Aquarius. Your ideas are from another planet! Knit a tiny alien? Sure, why not? A pair of scary zombies? No problem. An entire royal wedding, including church and guests? I thought you'd never ask. Nothing is impossible; it's so much fun being you.

Air sign Aquarius rules inventions and astrology—suggested project: an **electric-blue astronaut** (for space-age excitement).

POETIC PISCES

Yarn flows through your fingers as you weave it into a web of wonder, Pisces. Each piece sings of the sea, calls to the clouds, meanders into the mist—you personally connect to the power of nature with every creation. Some say you're a dreamer, a hopeless romantic, an artist—they're right.

Water sign Pisces rules the feet—suggested project: **silver slippers** (to dance in the moonlight).

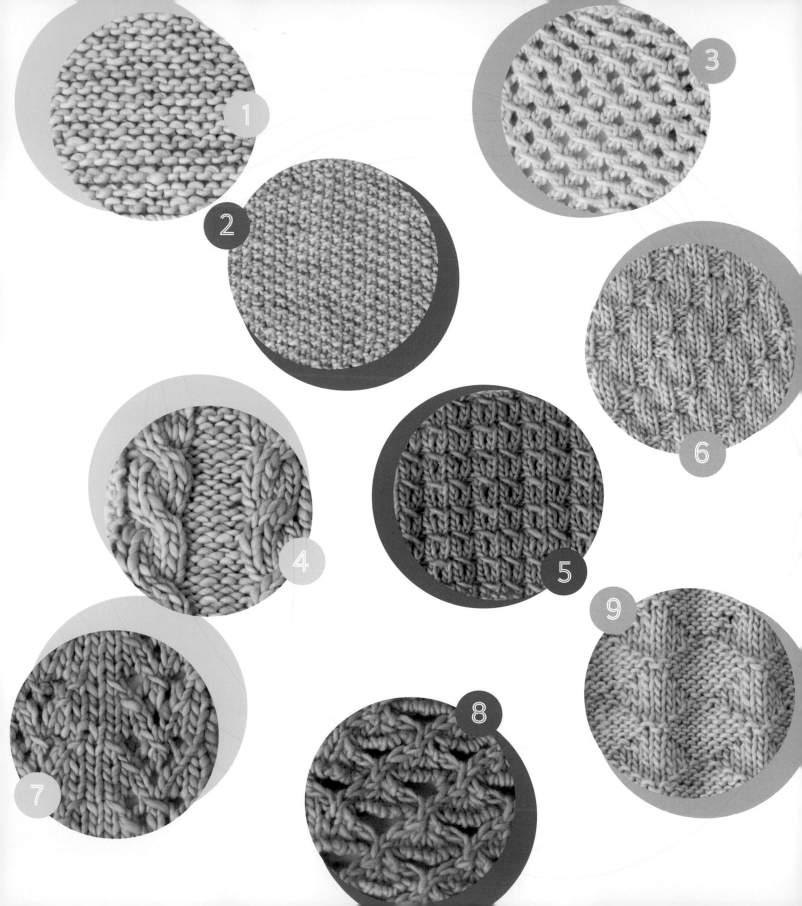

KNITTING & NUMEROLOGY, WITH DR. FELICIA BENDER, THE PRACTICAL NUMEROLOGIST

Knitting and crochet are both number-oriented, so it makes sense that numerology could resonate with stitchers. Through some of my own, personal research I came upon the work of Felicia Bender, PhD, aka the Practical Numerologist, who combines spirituality and numerology within her work with clients. Felicia was kind enough to share introductions to Life Path Numbers, which are based on your birth date and describe your traits, as well as potential lessons, challenges, and opportunities. The descriptions below just scratch the surface. If you're interested in learning more, please check out the Resources (page 206).

Since each number has a vibration, as do we and our actions, how about exploring the focus of your Life Path Number within your knitting practice? Along with each Life Path Number description below, I've included a swatch using stitch-pattern counts that correspond. Use your craft to channel your number's potential!

The 1 is the leader and is learning about independence and confidence. The 1 is connected with new opportunity, inspiration, new starts, initiation, standing alone, originality, courage, concentration, determination, and leadership.

#1 SWATCH
(Garter Stitch, using 1 stitch, repeated, every row)

CO 11 sts.

Row 1: K every stitch.

Repeat Row 1 for as many rows as desired (since all numbers can be multiplied by one, hence the leading number).

BO.

The 2 is a lover, not a fighter. The 2 is learning about love, patience, and diplomacy. The 2 is connected with love, emotional sensitivity, teamwork, cooperation, partnerships, details, serving group dynamics, harmony, and peace.

#2 SWATCH
(Seed Stitch, knits and purls, alternating every row, work in harmony with one another to create the seed pattern)

CO any multiple of 2.

Rows 1 and 2: *K1, p1; rep to end.

Repeat Rows 1 and 2 for any number of rows that is a multiple of 2.

BO.

HOW TO CALCULATE YOUR LIFE PATH NUMBER:

STEP 1
Begin with your full birth date number.

Example: January 7, 2002 (1-7-2-0-0-2)

STEP 2
Reduce the month, date, and year down to a single digit by first adding them together.

$1 + 7 + 2 + 0 + 0 + 2 = 12$

If the resulting number is a double digit, reduce it down again by adding the two digits.

$1 + 2 = 3$

Life Path Number = 3

The 3 is the communicator and is learning about creative self-expression and emotional sensitivity. The 3 is connected with joy, self-improvement, humor, artistic creativity, communication, performance, scattered focus, and dramatic emotional ups and downs.

#3 SWATCH

(Mesh Stitch, multiples of 3, connected by a stitch passed over, and open-weave symbolizing communication)

CO any multiple of 3.

Row 1: K2, *yo, sl 1, k2, psso; rep from * to last st, k1.

Rows 2 and 4: Purl.

Row 3: K1, *sl 1, k2, psso, yo; rep from * to the last 2 sts, k2.

Repeat Rows 1–4 for a multiple of 3 rows (e.g., 12, 24, etc.).

BO.

The 4 is the systems builder and is learning about stability, security, and effective process. The 4 is connected with material interests, structure, managing finances, creating lasting foundations, hard work, management, organization, efficiency, physical endurance, and limitations.

#4 SWATCH

(4-Stitch Cables, an intermediate stitch for born teachers, creating columns for stability)

SPECIAL STITCHES
Cable 4 Back – C4B
Cable 4 Front – C4F

CO any multiple of 8.

Row 1: *P2, k4, p2, rep from * to end.

Row 2: *K2, p4, k2, rep from * to end.

Row 3: Rep Row 1.

Row 4: Rep Row 2.

Row 5: *P2, C4B or C4F, p2, rep from * to end.

Row 6: Rep Row 2.

Repeat Rows 1–6 for a multiple of 4 rows (e.g., 24, 36, etc.).

BO.

The 5 is the freedom seeker and is learning about fearlessness, adventure, and managing positive change. The 5 is connected with sensuality, sales, sex, freedom, travel, communication, changes, flexibility, excitement, and adventure.

#5 SWATCH

(Double Mock Cable Rib, multiples of 5 creating openwork to symbolize communication and ribbing for flexibility)

CO any multiple of 5.

Row 1: *P1, k1, yf, k2, yf, k1; rep from * to end.

Row 2: *P6, k1; rep from * to end.

Row 3: *P1, [sl 1, k2, psso] twice; rep from * to end.

Row 4: *P4, k1; rep from * to end.

Repeat Rows 1–4 for 20 rows, or a multiple of 5 (ending on whatever row you need to).

BO.

The 6 is the nurturer and is learning about responsibility, home, and family. The 6 is connected with home, family, relationships, marriage, divorce, romance, responsibility, harmony, teaching, and justice.

#6 SWATCH

(Diagonal Rib, multiples of 6 all leaning on each other and connected by the pattern)

CO any multiple of 6.

Rows 1 and 3: *K4, p2; rep from * to end.

Rows 2 and 4: *K2, p4; rep from * to end.

Rows 5 and 7: K2, *p2, k4; rep from * to last 4 sts, p2, k2.

Rows 6 and 8: P2, *k2, p4; rep from * to last 4 sts, k2, p2.

Rows 9 and 11: *P2, k4; rep from * to end.

Rows 10 and 12: *P4, k2; rep from * to end.

Repeat Rows 1–12 for a multiple of 6 rows.

BO.

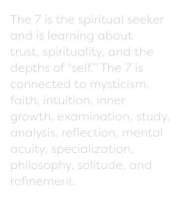

#7 SWATCH

(Arrow Lace, multiples of 7, open to intuition and pointing toward that which they seek)

CO any multiple of 7 sts.

Row 1: *K4, yo, k3; rep from * to end.

Row 2 and all WS rows: Purl.

Row 3: *K2, k2tog, yo, k1, yo, skpsso, k1; rep from * to end.

Row 5: *K1, k2tog, yo, sl 1 k2-psso, yo, skpsso; rep from * to end.

Row 6: Purl.

Repeat Rows 1–6 for a multiple of 7 rows, ending on a RS row.

BO on wrong side.

The 8 is the master of the material world and is learning about finances, empowerment, and authority. The 8 is connected to ethics, influence, money, business success (and failure), control, status, loss, gain, executive administration, management, ego, and personal power.

#8 SWATCH

(Grand Eyelet Lattice, multiples of 8, oversize, authoritative eyelets within a bed of a ladder for climbing toward success)

SPECIAL STITCHES
ssp2tog – slip, slip, purl 2 together

CO 24 sts.

Rows 1 and 5 (WS): Purl every st.

Row 2: *[K2 tog] twice, [yo] twice, [ssk] twice; rep from * to end.

Row 3: *Ssp2tog, [p1, k1] 3 times into the double yo, p2tog; rep from * to end.

Row 4: K1, *k6, k2tog but do not slip from needle; insert right-hand needle between the stitches just knitted together and knit the 1st stitch again, then slip both stitches from the needle together; rep from * to last 7 sts, k7.

Row 6: K4, *[k2tog] twice, [yo] twice, [ssk] twice; rep from * to last 4 sts, k4.

Row 7: P4, *ssp, [p1, k1] 3 times into the double yo, p2tog; rep from * to last 4 sts, p4.

Row 8: K3, *k2tog but do not slip from needle; insert right-hand needle between the stitches just knitted together and knit the 1st stitch again, then slip both stitches from the needle together, k6; rep from * to last 5 sts, k2tog but do not slip from needle; insert right-hand needle between the stitches just knitted together and knit the 1st stitch again, then slip both stitches from the needle together, k3.

Repeat Rows 1–8 until piece reaches desired length.

BO.

The 9 is the compassionate humanitarian and is learning about limited rewards, letting go, and philanthropy. The 9 is connected to unconditional love, humanitarianism, leadership by example, dramatic endings, emotional love, emotional crisis, the finer things in life, conclusions, compassion, magnetism, travel, idealism, charity, artistry, creativity, spirituality, romance, and forgiveness.

#9 SWATCH

(Plain Diamonds, multiple of 9; diamonds symbolize love, ethics, and character)

CO a multiple of 9 sts.

Row 1: K4, *p1, k8; rep from * to last 5 sts, p1, k4.

Rows 2 and 8: P3, *k3, P6; rep from * to last 6 sts, k3, p3.

Rows 3 and 7: K2, *p5, k4; rep from * last 7 sts, p5, k2.

Rows 4 and 6: P1, *k7, p2; rep from * to last 8 sts, k7, p1.

Row 5: Purl all sts.

Repeat Rows 1–8 until piece reaches desired length.

BO.

TWO

making

*Unexpected Home Decor, Go-To Gifts,
Must-Make Accessories, and
Inspo Projects to Feed Your Fiber-y Soul.*

THE
UNEXPECTED

Think outside the general gauge box. Play with shapes and methods in an unexpected way. Bring knit and crochet pieces into your home not just as a practicality (although I do love a snuggly blanket and pillow pop of color), but as conversation pieces. This section shows the juxtaposition of traditional craft and nonconformist art to create a look that feels less homemaker (not that there's anything wrong with that), more home-stunner!

MEGA CROCHET RUG

vickie howell

MATERIALS
3 bumps Plump & Co Chunky Merino Yarn (100% merino wool; 1 kg/55 m bump): 2 bumps White (A) and 1 bump Gray (B)

Size 35 mm crochet hook

FINISHED MEASUREMENTS
Approx. 42" (107 cm) circle

GAUGE
2 dc x 1 rnd = 4" (10 cm)

Note: This pattern is written in U.S. terms. See page 205 for U.K. conversion chart.

Another great yarn option: Loopy Mango Tough Loop.

DIRECTIONS

With A, ch 4; join rnd with a sl st.

Rnd 1: Ch 3 (counts a dc), 11 dc in center ring; with B, join rnd with a sl st in the top of beg ch-3—12 sts.

Cut A.

Rnd 2: With B, ch 3, dc in same st as ch, 2 dc in every st around; join rnd with a sl st in the top of beg ch-3—24 sts.

Rnd 3: Ch 3, *2 dc in next st, dc in next st; rep from * around, ending with a 2 dc; with A, join rnd with a sl st in the top of beg, ch-3—36 sts.

Cut B.

Rnd 4: With A, ch 3, *2 dc in next st, dc in next 2 sts; rep from * around, ending with 1 dc; join rnd with a sl st in the top of beg ch-3—48 sts.

Rnd 5: Ch 3, *2 dc in next st, dc in next 3 sts; rep from * around, ending with 1 dc; join rnd with a sl st in the top of beg ch-3—60 sts.

Rnd 6 (Picot edging): Ch 1, 2 sc in next st, *(sc, ch 3, sl st in 3rd ch from hook) in next st, sc in next st, (sc, ch 3, sl st in 3rd ch from hook), 2 sc in next st; rep from * around; join rnd with a sl st—23 picots.

FINISHING
Using fingers, weave in ends.

HOOP ART
andrea brinkley

ANDREA BRINKLEY, or Andy, was born and raised in South Africa and moved to the United States in her twenties. She lives and works in Charlotte, North Carolina, is the owner and designer of O&Y Studio, and sells her one-of-a-kind, wool-on-wool embroideries in her Etsy shop.

TIPS FOR EMBROIDERING ON SWEATERS

With some leftover yarns and threads, you can take an old cardigan from your closet or a thrift-shop bargain and completely make it over to resemble an expensive designer sweater. Here are a few tips for embellishment success:

1. Your woolen threads for embellishing should match the weight of the sweater's yarn. If they are too heavy or too thick, you run the risk of making holes in your sweater. Sock yarn or single strands of needlepoint yarn are perfect for fine gauge sweaters.

2. Be sure to use a needle with a diameter that closely matches the thickness of your yarn. If it's too small, the eye will be difficult to thread and the shank will not make a hole big enough for the yarn to travel through.

3. French knots and beads make great flower centers!

4. Hand-wash adorned sweaters and lay flat to dry to prevent potential felting caused by a washing machine.

MATERIALS

Beads, assorted sizes and shapes, for embellishments (optional)

Crochet hook

Decorative threads, assorted, for embellishments

Needles, tapestry and beading, in various sizes

Scissors

Sewing or beading thread

Wooden embroidery hoop

Wool, worsted weight, for background

Wool or wool blends, assorted colors and weights, for embroidery

Note: This pattern is written in U.S. terms. See page 205 for U.K. conversion chart.

GENERAL METHOD
DIRECTIONS

Step 1: Choose a hoop and background wool. Using a crochet hook that corresponds to the wool, crochet a circle.

Step 2: Either start with 4–5 crochet chains and connect them to make a ring or start with a magic ring and 4–5 chains.

Step 3: Sc 6 into the circle, going around and around, increasing by 6 sts every rnd to keep the circle flat.

Step 4: When your circle is half an inch smaller than your inner hoop, fasten off by cutting the wool and pulling it through the loop.

Step 5: Stitch the crocheted round into the inner circle of the hoop as if to mount it. It should be taut but not stretched too much.

Step 6: Apply the outer hoop and tighten it. You are ready to embroider the flowers.

Select an assortment of weights and colors of wool and use different embroidery stitches to represent various petals, leaves, and stems. Study either real flowers and buds or illustrations that you find in books, on wrapping paper, or online. Observe the shapes of the petals, number of petals, centers, shading, their stems and leaves. However you interpret the design, it is your unique art. There is no wrong way. It's literally like painting with a needle and thread!

Step 7 (optional): When you have completed the embroidery, you may want to embellish your piece with beads or decorative threads.

Completed hoops look wonderful in an eclectic collection of art, plates, and framed photos on a gallery wall.

MONDO CABLE WALL HANGING

vickie howell

MATERIALS

2 bumps Plump & Co Chunky Merino Yarn (100% merino wool; 1 kg/55 m bump): Midnight (A)

1 bump Plump & Co Chunky Merino Yarn Cheese Mini 2-ply (100% merino wool; 200 g/ 30 m bump): Grapefruit (B)

Size 45 mm needles

Pipe cleaner

1" (2.5 cm) x 36" (91 cm) wooden dowel

SIZE

Approx. 22" (56 cm) x 60" (152 cm), excluding hanger

GAUGE

9 sts = 4" (10 cm) Reverse Stockinette

SPECIAL STITCHES

CF6 = Cable 6 stitches

Slide first 3 stitches onto pipe cleaner (acting as an extra-long cable needle), let fall forward; knit next 3 stitches; knit 3 stitches off of pipe cleaner.

DIRECTIONS

With A, CO 14 sts.

Row 1: P4, k6, p4.

Row 2: K4, p6, k4.

Rows 3 and 4: Rep Rows 1 and 2.

Row 5: P4, CF6, p4.

Row 6: Rep Row 2.

Repeat Rows 1–6, twice more.

Repeat Rows 1–4, once more.

BO.

FINISHING

Weave in ends. Block if necessary.

Make Center Tassel Fringe:
Cut five 24" (61 cm) strands of B.

Hold strands together and fold in half.

Attach at centermost cable cross by sliding folded portion of strands under cross until a loop appears; feed strand ends through loop; pull snugly.

Unravel plies of strands.

Make Hanging Fringe:
Cut ten 62" (157.5 cm) strands of A.

Holding 2 strands together at a time, and using similar method to Tassel Fringe, attach 5 fringe bundles evenly across bottom edge of piece.

Optional Macramé Detail:
Using 6 strands at a time, make alternating square knots across hanging fringe as follows:

Holding 2 strands together, lay strands on the far right **over** the center 2 strands, and **under** the 2 strands on the far left side.

Bring strand on far left side **under** the center 2 strands, then up through loop created by the strand on the far right side.

Pull taut, but not tight.

Holding 2 strands together, lay strands on the far left **over** the center 2 strands, and **under** the 2 strands on the far right side.

Bring strand on far right side **under** the center 2 strands, then up through loop created by the strand on the far left side. Pull to complete knot.

Repeat process for as many square knots as desired.

Trim fringe so even.

Attach to Dowel:
Using fingers and strand of A, whipstitch top of piece to dowel.

Make Hanger:
Cut two 48" (122 cm) strands of A. Fold one strand in half and tie on, as for fringe, to one end of dowel. Repeat for other strand on opposite side.

Knot strands at top.

BOLD BASKETS

vickie howell

MATERIALS
1 bump hand-dyed
Independence Farmstead
Fibermill Texas Wool
(with core, approx. 125 yd)

Size U.S. 50 (25 mm)
crochet hook

GAUGE
Not important for
this project.

**FINISHED
MEASUREMENTS**
Large: 10" (25 cm) wide x 7"
(18 cm) tall

Small: 8" (20 cm) wide x 4"
(10 cm) tall

*Note: This pattern is
written in U.S. terms.
See page 205 for U.K.
conversion chart.*

*Another great yarn option:
Loopy Mango Big Loop.*

DIRECTIONS

For both sizes:
Ch 4, sl st in 1st ch to
form loop.

Rnd 1: Ch 1 (doesn't count
as st), 6 sc in center of loop;
join rnd with a sl st.

Rnd 2: Ch 1, *2sc in next st;
repeat from * around;
join rnd with a sl st—12 sts.

Rnd 3: Ch 1, *2sc in next
st, sc in next st; rep from *
around; join rnd with a sl
st—18 sts.

Large size only:
Rnd 4: Ch 1, *2sc in next st,
sc in next two sts; rep from
* around; join rnd with a sl
st—24 sts.

Both sizes:
Next Rnd: Ch1, sc in the BL
only of every st around; join
rnd with a sl st—18 (24) sts.

Next Rnd: Ch 1, sc in
every st around; join rnd
with a sl st.

For small size, rep last rnd
once more, for large size
rep three times more.

Fasten off.

FINISHING
Use fingers to weave
in ends.

GO-TO GIFTS

Giving is an important aspect of the knitters' zeitgeist. But what to gift? Some projects are no-brainers. You've gotta make 'em. You've gotta give 'em. Whether it's the on-trend, chunky cowl for your sister, slouchy beanie for your man, or wrist warmers for, well, everyone, I've designed some cool, simple (but not basic) versions for any (and every) occasion!

GO-TO GRADIENT SCARF

Moss Stitch is one of those patterns that is so pleasingly textural that any project using it looks richer for it. Meshed with a soft tweed yarn and the undulation of tonal color changes, though, the texture seems to come to life, making the Go-to Gradient Scarf just that: a must-make item that works for any gift-deserving gal or guy.

MATERIALS
2 hanks The Farmer's Daughter Fibers Craggy Tweed (85% superwash merino wool/15% NEP; 231 yd/100 g): 1 skein each in Pukuni (A) and Buffalo Gal (B)

Size U.S. 6 (4 mm) needles *or size needed to obtain gauge*

Tapestry needle

FINISHED MEASUREMENTS
Approx. 9" (23 cm) x 66" (168 cm)

GAUGE
18 sts x 20 rows = 4" (10 cm) in Moss Stitch

DIRECTIONS

With color A, CO 40 sts.

Rows 1 and 2: *K1, p1; rep from * to end.

Rows 3 and 4: *P1, k1; rep from * to end.

Rows 1–4 form Moss Stitch.

Work in Moss Stitch until piece measures 8½" (21.5 cm) from CO edge.

From here on, you're going to start fading the two colors in and out, while maintaining Moss Stitch as established. You can choose to follow the sequence below or alternate any way you'd like as long as you're mindful to divide the yardage up relatively evenly. Cut and rejoin unused color in between fade sections.

COLOR SEQUENCE:
2 rows in color B

2 rows in color A

Work in color B until piece measures 16½" (42 cm) from CO edge.

2 rows in color A

2 rows in color A

2 rows in color B

Work in color A until piece measures 25" (63.5 cm) from CO edge.

2 rows in color B

2 rows in color A

Work in color B until piece measures 33" (84 cm) from CO edge.

2 rows in color A

2 rows in color B

Work in color A until piece measures 39" (99 cm) from CO edge.

2 rows in color B

2 rows in color A

Work in color B until piece measures 46" (117 cm) from CO edge.

2 rows in color A

2 rows in color B

Work in color A until piece measures 52" (132 cm) from CO edge.

2 rows in color B

2 rows in color A

Work in color B until piece measures 58" (147 cm) from CO edge.

2 rows in color A

2 rows in color B

Work in color A until piece measures 62" (157.5 cm) from CO edge.

2 rows in color B

2 rows in color A

Work in color B until piece measures 66" (168 cm) from CO edge.

BO in patt st.

FINISHING
Weave in ends.

GO-TO CABLED MITTENS

A pair of chunky mittens puts cheer in even the coldest of days. Cables and hand-painted yarn make this set extra special. Knit and give them as a contribution to changing the old adage to say that in fact, warm hands equal a warm heart!

MATERIALS
1 skein Koigu Chelsea Merino (100% merino wool; 125 yd/100 g skein), in color: C718

Set of U.S. 9 (5.5 mm) double-pointed needles (dpns)—or size needed to obtain gauge

2 stitch markers, tapestry needle, cable needle (cn)

SIZES
One Size
Stretches to fit up to 9" (23 cm) palm circumference.

FINISHED MEASUREMENTS
8" (20 cm) circumference, 9½" (24 cm) length

GAUGE
14 sts x 18 rnds = 4" (10 cm) in Stockinette Stitch

SPECIAL STITCHES
C3/3R: Sl 3 sts to cn, hold back, k3; k3 from cn

C3/3F: Sl 3 sts to cn, hold front, k3; k3 from cn

Horseshoe Cable Pattern (worked in the round over 12 sts):

Rnds 1 and 2: K12.

Rnd 3: C3/3R, C3/3L.

Rnds 4–7: K12.

Rnd 8: C3/3R, C3/3L.

Repeat Rnds 1–8 for pattern.

DIRECTIONS

Note: Work the sts outside the 12-st cable panel in Reverse Stockinette Stitch (purl every round).

LEFT MITT

CUFF
CO 26 sts. Divide evenly among dpns; join for working in the rnd, being careful not to twist sts.

Rnds 1–10: *K1, p1; rep from * around.

BODY
Rnd 11: P4, pfb, p4, kfb, k7, kfb, p4, pfb, p2—30 sts.

Rnds 12–19: P9, work next 12 sts in Horseshoe Cable Pattern, p9.

Begin thumb gusset:
Rnd 20: P5, pm, M1, p1, M1, pm, p4, work 12 sts in Horseshoe cable panel, p around.

Rnd 21: Work in pattern as est (p to marker, sm, p to marker, sm, p4, work 12 sts in Horseshoe Cable Pattern, p around).

Rnd 22: P5, sm, M1, p to marker, M1, sm, work in pattern around—2 sts increased.

Rnd 23: Work in pattern as est.

Rnds 24–27: Rep Rnds 22 and 23, ending with Row 8 of Horseshoe Cable pattern—9 thumb sts between markers.

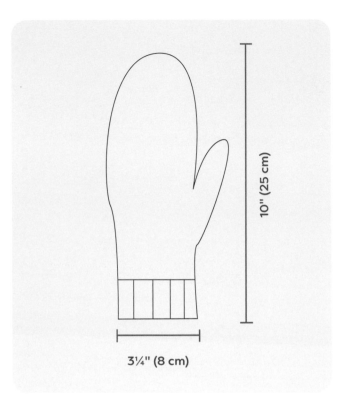

10" (25 cm)

3¼" (8 cm)

Rnds 28–33: Work in pattern as est.

Rnd 34: P5, remove marker, sl 9 thumb sts onto waste yarn, remove marker, M1, p4, work 12 sts in Horseshoe Cable panel, purl around—30 sts.

TOP OF MITT

Rnd 1: [P2tog] 4 times, p1, [k2tog] 6 times, p1, [p2tog] 4 times—16 sts.

Rnd 2: P5, k6, p5.

Rnd 3: [P2tog] 2 times, [k2tog] 4 times, ssk, [p2tog] 2 times—10 sts.

Rnd 4: Purl around.

Cut yarn, leaving a long tail. Thread through live sts. Pull tight to close hole at top of mitt, fasten off.

THUMB

Place thumb sts evenly on dpns, picking up 2 sts in the gap. Join for working in the rnd—11 sts.

Work in Reverse Stockinette Stitch (purl every rnd) until thumb measures 2" (5 cm) on the side closest to palm.

Next Rnd: [P2tog] 5 times, p1—6 sts.

Next Rnd: Purl around.

Last Rnd: [P2tog] 3 times—3 sts.

Cut yarn, leaving a long tail. Thread through live sts.

Pull tight to close hole at top of thumb, fasten off.

RIGHT MITT

Cast on and work as for Left Mitt to end of Rnd 19.

Begin thumb gusset:
Rnd 20: P9, work 12 sts in Horseshoe Cable panel, p2, pm, M1, p1, M1, pm, purl around.

Rnd 21: Work in pattern as est (p9, work 12 sts in Horseshoe Cable panel, p2, sm, p to marker, sm, purl around).

Rnd 22: Work in pattern as est to marker, sm, M1, p to marker, M1, sm, purl around—2 sts increased.

Rnd 23: Work in pattern as est.

Rnds 24–27: Rep Rnds 22 and 23, ending with Row 8 of Horseshoe Cable pattern—9 thumb sts between markers.

Rnds 28–33: Work in pattern as est.

Rnd 34: P9, work 12 sts in Horseshoe Cable panel, p2, remove marker, sl 9 thumb sts onto waste yarn, remove marker, M1, purl around—30 sts.

Work top of mitt and thumb as for Left Mitt.

FINISHING

Weave in ends.

GO-TO MARKET BAG

A market bag is a great gift option for warmer months, for someone whom you may not know well enough to know their wearables taste, or for that person who has everything (after all, you can never have too many shopping bags).

MATERIALS
1 ball Schoppel-Wolle Zauberball Cotton (100% cotton; 462 yd/ 100 g ball): color #2339

Size U.S. G (4 mm) crochet hook

Tapestry needle

FINISHED MEASUREMENTS
Approx. 8" x 15" (20.5 cm x 38 cm), excluding handles

GAUGE
Not important for this project

Note: This pattern is written in U.S. terms. See page 205 for U.K. conversion chart.

DIRECTIONS

BOTTOM
Leaving long tail for seaming, ch 85. Join rnd, taking care not to twist.

Rnds 1–5: Ch 2 (counts as hdc), hdc in next st and every st around; join rnd with a sl st—85 sts.

BODY
Rnd 6: Ch 4 (counts as tr), tr, ch 3, sk 3, *2 tr, ch 3, sk 3; rep from * to end; join rnd with a sl st—34 tr, 17 ch-3 sps.

Rnds 7 and 8: Ch 2, hdc in next st and every st around; join rnd with a sl st.

Repeat Rnds 6–8, eight times more.

Repeat Rnd 7 three times more.

Fasten off.

HANDLES

Measure 2" (5 cm) in from one edge of bag. Rejoin yarn.

Rnd 1: Ch 2, hdc 5; turn.

Repeat Rnd 1 until piece measures 12" (30.5 cm).

Fasten off, leaving long tail for seaming.

Flip bag over and repeat process for opposite side.

FINISHING

Using tapestry needle and tails, seam up bottom and sew loose handles to bag (2" [5 cm] from opposite side of bag top from where handles began).

Weave in ends.

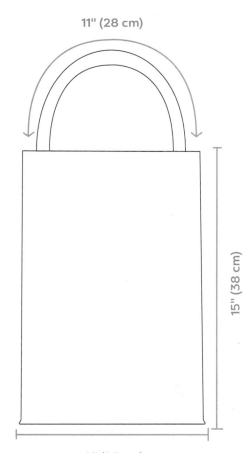

11" (28 cm)

15" (38 cm)

9" (23 cm)

GO BIG!

Want a bigger bag? Simply go up in yarn weight and hook size. This version is made with lace-weight, so go grander by considering sport, worsted, or even chunky weight yarns!

GO-TO SLOUCHY BEANIE

A slouchy beanie is a hat with attitude. The extra length allows for a bit of style swagger while also lending extra warmth at the base of the head where the extra fabric should gather. This version has twisted stitches for texture, ribbing for stretch, and the occasional crossed stitch for interest. This hat makes a great unisex gift for those cool kids (or kids at heart) on your list!

MATERIALS
3 hanks Malabrigo Worsted (100% kettle-dyed merino wool; 210 yd/100 g): 1 each in Polar Morn (A), Water Green (B), and Frank Ochre (C)

Size U.S. 8 (5 mm), 16" (40 cm) circular needle—*or size needed to obtain gauge*

Set of size U.S. 8 (5 mm) double-pointed needles (dpns)—*or size needed to obtain gauge*

Stitch marker, tapestry needle, cable needle (cn)

SIZES
S/M (L/XL)

Stretches to fit up to 22 (24)" (56 [61] cm) head

FINISHED MEASUREMENTS
18 (19)" (46 [48] cm) circumference, unstretched; 10" (25 cm) height

GAUGE
20 sts x 22 rnds = 4" (10 cm) in Twisted Rib Stitch (k1tbl, p1), unstretched

SPECIAL STITCHES
T1/2L: Sl 1 st onto cn, hold to front, p1, k1tbl, k1tbl from cn.

DIRECTIONS

With color A, CO 90 (96) sts. Join for working in the rnd, being careful not to twist sts. Pm indicating beg of rnd.

Rnds 1–7: *K1tbl, p1; rep from * around.

Cut color A; join color B.

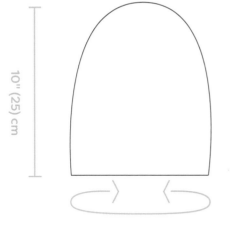

10" (25) cm

16 (17)" (40.5 [43] cm)

Rnds 8–14: *K1tbl, p1; rep from * around.

Cut color B; join color C.

Rnds 15 and 16: *K1tbl, p1; rep from * around.

Rnd 17: *T1/2L, p1, k1tbl, p1; rep from * around.

Rnds 18 and 19: *K1tbl, p1; rep from * around.

Rnds 20–22: Rep Rnds 17–19.

Cut color C; join color A.

Rnds 23–30: *K1tbl, p1; rep from * around.

Cut color A; join color B.

Rnd 31–38: Rep Rnds 15–22.

Cut color B; join color C.

Rnds 39–46: *K1tbl, p1; rep from * around.

Cut color C; join color A.

Rnd 47–54: Rep Rnds 15–21.

Rnd 55: *K1tbl, p1; rep from * around.

Repeat last rnd until piece measures 10" (25 cm) from cast-on edge.

BO in patt st, leaving long tail for seaming.

FINISHING
Close hat as follows:

1. With tapestry needle and tail, insert through center front and back (joining front and back at center); make a stitch.

2. Pinch side edges to the same center point and stitch through both thicknesses. The top of the beanie will now be in a cross formation.

3. Continue in this manner, pinching the opposite edges and stitching them together at the center until top of hat is completely closed.

Fasten off. Weave in ends.

GO-TO WRIST WARMERS

Fingerless gloves are mainstay pieces for anyone who types on a keyboard in an over-air-conditioned room, sends texts from a phone while standing on a chilly street, and yes, knits on a patio during a winter retreat. This pair is knit in cashmere with petite cable detailing on the cuffs and thumbs, which makes them not only a practical gift but a luxurious one.

MATERIALS

1 ball Clinton Hill Cashmere Company Bespoke (100% Italian cashmere; 99 yd/50 g): French Grey

Set of size U.S. 8 (5 mm) double-pointed needles (dpns)—*or size needed to obtain gauge*

2 stitch markers, tapestry needle, waste yarn, cable needle (cn)

FINISHED MEASUREMENTS

8" (20 cm) circumference, 8" (20 cm) length

GAUGE

16 sts x 24 rnds = 4" (10 cm) in Stockinette Stitch

SPECIAL STITCHES

C2F: Sl 1 st onto cn, hold front, k1; k1 from cn.

C2B: Sl 1 st onto cn, hold back, k1; k1 from cn.

DIRECTIONS

LEFT WRIST WARMER

CUFF
CO 32 sts. Divide evenly among dpns; join for working in the rnd, being careful not to twist sts.

Rnd 1: Knit.

Rnd 2: *C2F, C2B; rep from * around.

Rnd 3: Knit.

Repeat Rnds 2 and 3 seven times more.

BODY
Rnds 1–4: Knit.

BEGIN THUMB GUSSET
Rnd 5: K7, pm, k1, pm, k around.

Rnd 6: K to marker, sm, M1, k to marker, M1, sm, k around—2 sts increased.

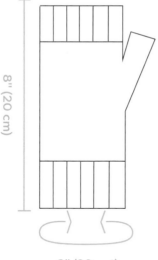

8" (20 cm)

8" (20 cm)

Rnd 7: Knit around.

Rnds 8 and 9: Rep Rnds 6 and 7.

Rnd 10: K to marker, sm, M1, k1, C2F, C2B, M1, sm, k around—2 sts increased.

Rnd 11: Knit around.

Rnd 12: K to marker, sm, M1, k2, C2F, C2B, k1, M1, sm, k around—9 thumb sts between markers.

Rnd 13: Knit around.

Rnd 14: K to marker, sm, k3, C2F, C2B, k2, sm, k around.

Rnd 15: Knit around.

Rnds 16–21: Rep Rnds 14 and 15.

Rnd 22: K to marker, remove marker, sl 9 thumb sts onto waste yarn, remove marker, M1, k to end of round—32 sts.

Rnds 23–26: Knit around.

Rnd 27: *C2F, C2B; rep from * around.

Rnd 28: Knit around.

Rnds 29–32: Rep Rnds 27 and 28.

BO all sts loosely.

THUMB

Place thumb sts evenly on dpns, picking up 2 sts in the gap. Join for working in the rnd—11 sts.

Rnd 1: K to cable sts, C2F, C2B, k around.

Rnd 2: Knit around.

Rnds 3 and 4: Rep Rnds 1 and 2.

BO all sts loosely.

RIGHT WRIST WARMER

Cast on and work same as for Left Wrist Warmer to end of Body Rnd 4.

BEGIN THUMB GUSSET

Rnd 5: K24, pm, k1, pm, k around.

Rnd 6: K to marker, sm, M1, k to marker, M1, sm, k around—2 sts increased.

Rnd 7: Knit around.

Rnds 8 and 9: Rep Rnds 6 and 7.

Rnd 10: K to marker, sm, M1, C2F, C2B, k1, sm, k around.

Rnd 11: Knit around.

Rnd 12: K to marker, sm, M1, k1, C2F, C2B, k2, M1, sm, k around—9 thumb sts between markers.

Rnd 13: Knit around.

Rnd 14: K to marker, sm, k2, C2F, C2B, k3, sm, k around.

Rnd 15: Knit around.

Rnds 16–21: Rep Rnds 14 and 15.

Rnds 22–32: Work same as for Left Wrist Warmer.

THUMB

Work same as for Left Wrist Warmer.

FINISHING

Weave in ends. Soak in cool water and wool wash and block to measurements.

GO-TO SLIPPER SOCKS

Retro-chic cozy is the name of these slippers' game! That favorite be-pommed sock from the seventies lives a new life, reborn as a thicker slipper. Make these for Mom, Nana, friends, or that roommate whose feet never seem to warm up. Pom-pom peds forever!

MATERIALS
2 balls Valley Yarns Valley Superwash Color by Vickie Howell (100% superwash extra-fine merino; 97 yd/50g): 1 each in #305 Boho Blue (A), #303 Daquiri Ice (B)

Set of size U.S. 7 (4.5 mm) double-pointed needles (dpns)—*or size needed to obtain gauge*

Tapestry needle, stitch holder

SIZES
Women's S (M, L)

FINISHED MEASUREMENTS
8 (8, 9)" (20 [20, 23] cm) circumference

9 (9½, 10)" (23 [24, 25] cm) length

GAUGE
18 sts x 24 rnds = 4" (10 cm) in Stockinette Stitch

DIRECTIONS (MAKE 2)

With color A, CO 36 (36, 39) sts.

Rnds 1–4: *Ktbl, p2; rep from * around.

Rnd 5: Knit around.

Size L only:
Rnd 6: K19, M1, k around—40 sts.

ALL SIZES
Cut color A; join B.

Rnds 6 and 7: Knit around.

Note: The heel is worked back and forth in rows.

HEEL FLAP
You will now be working across the first 18 (18, 20) sts of the round. Put the remaining sts on a stitch holder.

Row 1 (RS): *Sl1, k1; rep from * to end.

Row 2 (WS): Sl1, p to end.

Repeat Rows 1 and 2 for 8 (9, 10) more times.

TURN HEEL
Row 1 (RS): Sl1, k10 (10, 12), ssk, k1. Turn.

Row 2 (WS): Sl 1, p4 (4, 6), p2tog, p1. Turn.

Row 3: Sl 1, k5 (5, 7), ssk, k1. Turn.

Row 4: Sl 1, p6 (6, 8), p2tog, p1. Turn.

Row 5: Sl 1, k7 (7, 9), ssk, k1. Turn.

Row 6: Sl 1, p8 (8, 10), p2tog, p to end. Turn.

Size L only:
Row 7: Sl 1, k10, ssk, k1. Turn.

Row 8: Sl 1, p10, p2tog, p1. Turn.

GUSSET

Set-up Rnd: Needle (N) 1: Knit heel sts, PU and k 11 (13, 15) sts along one side of flap; Needle 2: k 18 (18, 20) instep sts; Needle 3: PU and k 11 (13, 15) sts along other side of flap; k 9 (9, 10) heel sts. This is new beginning of rnd. Second half of heel sts can be worked and redistributed to Needle 1.

Join color A but don't cut color B.

Rnd 1: With color B, N1: k to 3 sts before end of needle, k2tog, k1; N2: k all sts; N3: k1, ssk, k to end of rnd—2 sts decreased.

Rnd 2: With color A, knit around.

Repeat Rnds 1–2 until 36 (36, 40) sts remain.

FOOT

Rnd 1: *K1 with A, k1 with B; rep from * around.

Rnd 2: With B, knit around.

Rnd 3: *K1 with B, k1 with A; rep from * around.

Rnd 4: With A, knit around.

Rnds 5–8: Rep Rnds 1–4.

Rnd 9: Rep Rnd 1.

Rnds 10 and 11: With B, knit.

Rnd 12: Rep Rnd 3.

Cut color A.

With color B, work in Stockinette Stitch (knit all rnds) until foot measures 7 (7½, 8)" (18 [19, 20] cm) from heel.

Cut color B; join color A.

TOE

Rnd 1: N1: k to last 3 sts, k2tog, k1; N2: k1, ssk, k to last 3 sts, k2tog, k1; N3: k1, ssk, k to end—4 sts decreased.

Rnd 2: Knit.

Repeat Rnds 1 and 2 until 12 (12, 12) sts remain. Cut yarn, leaving long tail.

Distribute first 6 sts and last 6 sts on N1 and N2. Holding needles parallel, graft the sts together using the Kitchener Stitch.

FINISHING

Using preferred method and both colors A and B, make 2 pom-poms. Sew pom-poms onto sock cuffs.

Weave in ends.

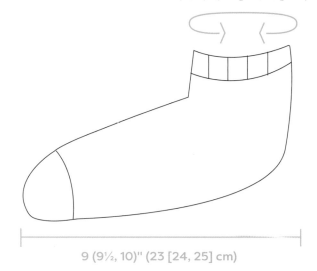

8 (8, 9)" (20 [20, 23] cm)

9 (9½, 10)" (23 [24, 25] cm)

GO-TO GRANNY BABY BLANKET

I can't remember a time when I wasn't gaga for granny squares. They're the first thing I learned to crochet and continue to be one of my go-to choices when I want a little batch of sweetness served up with a square construction. I say, start 'em while they're young; make baby's first gift a chunky, comfy granny square blankie. Oh, and bonus: this blanket is crocheted with a large hook using Super Bulky yarn, so you may actually finish it before the wee one starts walking!

MATERIALS

10 balls Valley Yarns Valley Superwash Super Bulky Color by Vickie Howell (100% superwash wool; 55 yd/100 g): 5 balls #208 Pink Flamingo (A), 2 balls #205 Boss Byzanthium (B), 1 ball #207 Astroturf (C), 2 balls #202 Moontower Mustard (D)

Size U.S. N/P (9 mm) crochet hook

Large-eye tapestry needle

FINISHED MEASUREMENTS

Approx. 36" (91 cm) square

GAUGE

Not important for this project.

Note: This pattern is written in U.S. terms. See page 205 for U.K. conversion chart.

DIRECTIONS

With color A, ch 6. Join with a sl st in first ch to form a ring.

Rnd 1: Ch 3 (counts as dc here and throughout), 2 dc in ring, [ch 3, 3 dc in ring] 3 times, ch 3; join with sl sl in 3rd ch of beginning ch-3—4 dc clusters, 4 ch-3 sp.

Rnd 2: Ch 4 (counts as dc and ch-1 sp here and throughout), *(3 dc, ch 3, 3 dc) in next corner ch-3 sp, ch 1; rep from * 2 more times, (3 dc, ch 3, 2 dc) in first corner ch-3 sp, ch 1; join with a sl st in 3rd chain of beginning ch-4—8 dc clusters, 8 ch-3 sp.

Rnd 3: Ch 3, 2dc in same ch-1 sp, ch 1, *(3dc, ch 3, 3 dc) in next corner ch-3 sp, ch 1, 3 dc in next ch-1 sp, ch

1; rep from * 2 more times, 3 dc in next ch-1 sp, ch 1, (3 dc, ch 3, 3 dc) in last corner ch-3 sp, ch 1; join with a sl st in 3rd chain of beginning ch-3—12 dc clusters.

Rnd 4: Sl st in next ch-1 sp, ch 3, 2 dc in same ch-1 sp, ch 1, *(3 dc, ch 3, 3 dc) in next corner ch-3 sp, ch 1**, [(3dc, ch 1) in next ch-1 sp] twice; rep from * 3 more times, ending last rep at **, (3dc, ch 1) in next ch-1 sp; join with a sl st in 3rd ch of beginning ch-3—16 dc clusters.

Rnd 5: Sl st in next ch-1 sp, ch 3, 2 dc in same ch-1 sp, ch 1, *(3 dc, ch 3, 3 dc) in corner ch-3 sp, ch 1**, (3dc, ch 1) in each ch-1 sp to next corner; rep from * 3 more times, join with a sl st in 3rd ch of beginning ch-3—20 dc clusters.

Cut color A; join color B.

Rnds 6–7: Rep Rnd 5—28 dc clusters.

Cut color B; join color C.

Rnd 8: Rep Rnd 5—32 dc clusters.

Cut color C; join color D.

Rnd 9: Rep Rnd 5—36 dc clusters.

Cut color D; join color A.

Rnds 10–13: Rep Rnd 5—52 dc clusters.

Cut color A; join color B.

Rnd 14: Rep Rnd 5—56 dc clusters.

Cut color B; join color C.

Rnd 15: Rep Rnd 5—60 dc clusters.

Cut color C; join color D.

Rnd 16: Rep Rnd 5—64 dc clusters.

EDGING
Cut color D; join color A.

Last Rnd: Ch 1 (counts as sc), *sc in each st to corner ch-3 sp, (sc in first ch-1, 3 sc in next ch-1, sc in next ch-1); rep from * 3 more times, sc in each st to end of rnd, join with a sl st in beginning ch-1.

Fasten off.

FINISHING
Weave in ends.

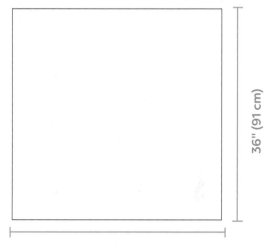

36" (91 cm)

36" (91 cm)

GO-TO CHUNKY COWL

If you're looking to churn out gorgeous, textural gifts in a short amount of time, then a slipped-stitch, spiral ribbed, chunky cowl is your answer. Fun, fast, and fab—this project is pretty much the trifecta of handmade holiday goodness!

MATERIALS
1 hank Malabrigo Rasta (100% hand-dyed merino wool; 90 yd/150 g): Frank Ochre

Size U.S. 13/9 mm, 24" circular needle

Stitch marker

SIZE
One Size

FINISHED MEASUREMENTS
25" (64 cm) circumference x 10½" (27 cm) tall

GAUGE
11 sts x 8 rows = 4" (10 cm) in Spiral Rib

DIRECTIONS

CO 57 sts; join, being careful not to twist sts. Place marker for beg of rnd.

Rnd 1: *P2, sl 1; rep from * around.

Rnds 2: *P2, k1; rep from * around.

Rnds 3–6: Rep Rnds 1–2.

Rnd 7: Sl 1, *p2, sl 1; rep from * around, end p2.

Rnd 8: K1, *p2, k1; rep from * around, end p2.

Rnds 9–12: Rep Rnds 7–8

Rnd 13: P1, *sl 1, p2, rep from * around, end sl 1, p1.

Rnd 14: P1, *k1, p2; rep from * around, end k1, p1.

Rnds 15–18: Rep Rnds 13–14.

Repeat Rnds 1–18 once more.

Repeat Rnds 1–6 once more.

BO in patt st.

FINISHING
Weave in ends.

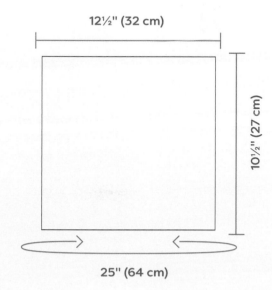

12½" (32 cm)

10½" (27 cm)

25" (64 cm)

GO-TO CHUNKY HAT

Need a last-minute gift? Know someone with a kicky personality who loves a charming chapeau? This hat's got you (or them, as the case may be) covered! Made with bulky yarn and using a quick-knitted mock cable and eyelet stitch, this beanie can be made in an evening. Top it off with a faux-fur pom-pom, wrap it up, and this present becomes a party in a box!

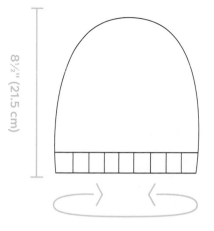

8½" (21.5 cm)

18 (19½") (36 [49.5] cm)

MATERIALS
1 skein Spun Right Round Big Rad Bulky (80% superwash merino wool, 20% nylon; 76 yd/100 g): Rumble in Brighton

Size U.S. 11 (8 mm) 16" (40 cm) circular needle—*or size needed to obtain gauge*

Set of size U.S. 11 (8 mm) double-pointed needles (dpns)—*or size needed to obtain gauge*

Stitch marker, large-eyed tapestry needle, faux fur pom-pom (optional, sample shown with 3½" [9 cm] pom-pom)

SIZES
S/M (L/XL)

Stretches to fit up to 22 (24)" (56 [61 cm]) head.

FINISHED MEASUREMENTS
18 (19½)" (46 [49.5] cm) circumference, 8½" (21.5) cm tall

GAUGE
10 sts x 14 rnds = 4" (10 cm) in pattern stitch

DIRECTIONS

CO 48 (52) sts. Join for working in the rnd, being careful not to twist sts. Pm indicating beg of rnd.

BRIM
Rnds 1–6: *K2, p2; rep from * around.

BODY
Size S/M, Rnd 7: K12, M1, k24, M1, k around—50 sts.
Size L/XL, Rnd 7: K9, [M1, k17] twice, M1, k around—55 sts.

Rnd 8: *Sl 1, k2, psso, p2; rep from * around—30 (33) sts.

Rnd 9: *[K1, yo, k1] into next st, p2; rep from * around—50 (55) sts.

Rnds 10 and 11: *K3, p2; rep from * around.

Pattern stitch established.

Rep Rnds 8–11 three times more, then rep Rnd 8 once more.

CROWN
Rnd 1: *[K1, yo, k1] into next st, p2tog; rep from * around—40 (44) sts.

Rnd 2: K3, p1; rep from * around.

Rnd 3: *Sl 1, k2tog, psso, p1; rep from * around—20 (22) sts.

Rnd 4: *[K1, yo, k1] into next st, p1; rep from * around—40 (44) sts.

Rnd 5: *K2tog, k1, p1; rep from * around—30 (33) sts.

Rnd 6: *K2, p1; rep from * around.

Rnd 7: *K2tog, p1; rep from * around—20 (22) sts.

Rnd 8: *K1, p1; rep from * around.

Rnd 9: *K2tog; rep from * around—10 (11) sts.

FINISHING
Cut yarn, leaving long tail. Thread yarn through live sts. Pull tight to close hole at top of hat, fasten off, and weave in ends.

Sew on optional pompom.

THE
CONTRIBUTORS

My love affair with knit- and crochetwear design has just as much to do with the amazing designers I'm a fan of as it does the time spent designing myself. It takes a village to perpetuate creativity, and the artists in the pages ahead do just that. This section is filled with accessory projects that kick up the skill level a bit and aim to inspire a lot!

MAGANA HI-LOW VEST

paula pereira

PAULA PEREIRA is a knitwear designer who believes that inspiration comes from people and nature. She loves to work with yarn and needles as tools to transform daily life inspirations into garments and accessories. She lives in São Paulo with her husband, two dogs, and tons of beautiful fibers.

The combination of interesting—biased fabric on the fronts and the upper back creates the perfect angles for shaping shoulders—and the pairing of a gorgeous speckled yarn with a furry brushed mohair adds a Boho look to this cozy-cool vest. Magana is a perfect layering piece for any wardrobe!

MATERIALS

2 (2, 3, 3, 3, 3) hanks La Bien Aimee Merino Singles (100% merino wool; 400 yd/100 g): Romance (MC)

5 (6, 6, 7, 7, 8) hanks Blue Sky Fibers Brushed Suri (67% baby Suri alpaca, 22% fine merino, 11% bamboo; 142 yd/100 g): #905 Earl Grey (CC)

Size U.S. 7 (4.5mm) 32" (80 cm) circular needle

2 size U.S. 8 (5mm) 32" (80 cm) circular needles

Adjust needle size if necessary to obtain the correct gauge.

Stitch markers, tapestry needle, long stitch holder or waste yarn

FINISHED BUST SIZE

39 (42, 46¾, 49¾, 52¾, 57½)"/99 (106.5, 118, 126.5, 134, 145.5) cm

To fit bust 32 (36, 40, 44, 48, 52)"/81.5 (91.5, 101.5, 112, 122, 132) cm with 4"–7" of + ease. Sample in size Small.

GAUGE

18 sts and 24 rows in 4" (10 cm) with double-held yarn and bigger needles in Stockinette Stitch, after blocking

NOTES

The vest is worked flat from the bottom up. The front stitches are worked in biased Stockinette Stitch fabric. Slip stitches purlwise with yarn in back except where indicated otherwise. For the 2 x 2 Rib with 2 yarns, the MC

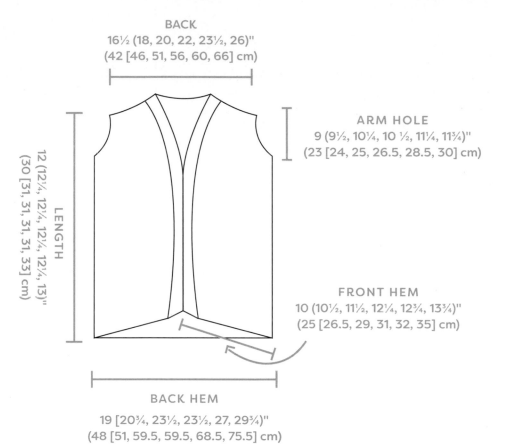

BACK
16½ (18, 20, 22, 23½, 26)"
(42 [46, 51, 56, 60, 66] cm)

LENGTH
12 (12¼, 12¼, 12¼, 12¼, 13)"
(30 [31, 31, 31, 31, 33] cm)

ARM HOLE
9 (9½, 10¼, 10 ½, 11¼, 11¾)"
(23 [24, 25, 26.5, 28.5, 30] cm)

FRONT HEM
10 (10½, 11½, 12¼, 12¾, 13¾)"
(25 [26.5, 29, 31, 32, 35] cm)

BACK HEM
19 [20¾, 23½, 23½, 27, 29¾)"
(48 [51, 59.5, 59.5, 68.5, 75.5] cm)

is La Bien Aimee Merino Singles and CC is La Bien Aimee Merino Singles and Blue Sky Fibers Brushed Suri DK held together. The yarns are held together to work in Stockinette Stitch.

PATTERN STITCHES
2 x 2 Rib with 2 yarns, La Bien Aimee Merino Singles as MC and La Bien Aimee Merino Singles and Blue Sky Fibers Brushed Suri DK held together as CC (multiple of 4 + 2 sts):

Row 1: *With MC, k2, with CC, p2, rep from * to last 2 sts, with MC, k2.

Row 2: *With MC, p2, with CC, k2, rep from * to last 2 sts, with MC, p2.

Repeat last 2 rows.

Stockinette Stitch (any number of sts):

Row 1 (RS): K all sts.

Row 2 (WS): P all sts.

Repeat last 2 rows.

BODY
With one strand each of MC and CC and smaller needles, using the Long Tail CO method, CO 206 (222, 246, 262, 278, 302) sts. Work in 2 X 2 Rib st (see Pattern Stitches) for 16 rows, ending with a WS row.

Change to larger needles and St st.

Set-up Row (RS): [K2, p2] 4 times, k1, pm, k 43 (47, 53, 57, 61, 67), pm, k 86 (94, 106, 114, 122, 134), pm, k 43 (47, 53, 57, 61, 67), pm, k1 [p2, k2] 3 times, p2, sl2 wyib.

Next Row (WS): [P2, k2] 4 times, p1, sm, p to last marker, sm, p1, [k2, p2] 3 times, k2, sl2 wyif.

Next Row (RS): [K2, p2] 4 times, k1, sm, M1R, k to 2 sts before next marker, k2tog, sm, k to next marker, sm, ssk, k to next marker, M1L, sm, k1, [p2, k2] 3 times, p2, sl2 wyib.

Next Row (WS): [P2, k2] 4 times, p1, sm, p to last marker, sm, p1, [k2, p2] 3 times, k2, sl2 wyif.

Repeat last 2 rows for 26 (27, 27, 27, 27, 28) more times—54 (56, 56, 56, 56, 60) rows total.

SHAPE ARMHOLES
Set-up Row (RS): [K2, p2] 4 times, k1, sm, M1R, k to 6 sts before next marker, k2tog, k1, BO 3 (3, 3, 3, 3, 3) sts, remove marker, BO 3 (3, 3, 3, 3, 3) sts, k to 3 sts before next marker, BO 3 (3, 3, 3, 3, 3) sts, remover marker, BO 3 (3, 3, 3, 3, 3) sts, ssk, k to next marker, M1L, sm, k1, [p2, k2] 3 times, p2, sl1 wyib—12 sts dec'd.

Transfer 57 (61, 67, 71, 75, 81) Right Front sts and 80 (88, 100, 108, 116, 128) Back sts onto a holder or waste yarn.

LEFT FRONT

Next Row (WS): [P2, k2] 4 times, p1, sm, p to 1 sts before end, sl1 wyif.

Dec Row (RS): Slip the first 2 sts and pass the first st over the second (this counts as first BO), BO 1, ssk, k to marker, M1L, sm, k1 [p2, k2] 3 times, p2, sl2 wyib—2 sts dec'd, 55 (59, 65, 69,73, 79) sts rem.

Next Row (WS): [P2, k2] 4 times, p1, sm, p to 1 sts before end, sl1 wyif.

Sizes XL and XXL only:
Repeat last 2 rows—55 (59, 65, 69, 71, 77) sts rem.

All sizes:
Dec Row: Slip the first 2 sts and pass the first st over the second (this counts as first BO), ssk, k to marker, M1L, sm, k1 [p2, k2] 3 times, p2, sl2 wyib—1 st dec'd, 54 (58, 64, 68, 70, 76) sts rem.

Next Row (WS): [P2, k2] 4 times, p1, sm, p to 1 st before end, sl1 wyif.

Sizes M and L only:
Repeat last 2 rows. 54 (58, 63, 67, 70, 76) sts rem.

All sizes:
Next Row (RS): K1, ssk, k to marker, M1L, sm, k1 (p2, k2) 3 times, p2, sl2 wyib.

Next Row (WS): [P2, k2] 4 times, p1, sm, p to 1 sts before end, sl1 wyif.

Repeat last 2 rows a further 24 (25, 27, 28, 30, 31) times—50 (52, 56, 58, 62, 64) rows total.

Transfer the 54 (58, 63, 67, 70, 76) left front sts onto a holder or waste yarn. Break yarn leaving a 6" (15 cm) tail.

RIGHT FRONT

With RS facing, attach yarn and work as follows.

Next Row: [K2, p2] 4 times, k1, sm, M1R, k to last 3 sts, k2tog, sl1 wyib.

Dec Row (WS): Slip the first 2 sts and pass the first st over the second (this counts as first BO), BO 1 (1, 1, 1, 1, 1) st, p to marker, sm, p1, [k2, p2] 3 times, k2, sl2 wyif—2 sts dec'd, 55 (59, 65, 69,73, 79) sts rem.

Next Row (RS): [K2, p2] 4 times, k1, sm, M1R, k to last 3 sts, k2tog, sl1 wyib.

Sizes XL and XXL only:
Repeat last 2 rows once more—55 (59, 65, 69, 71, 77) sts rem.

All sizes
Dec Row: Slip the first 2 sts and pass the first st over the second (this counts as first BO), p to marker, sm, p1, [k2, p2] 3 times, k2, sl2 wyif—1 st dec'd, 54 (58, 64, 68, 70, 76) sts rem.

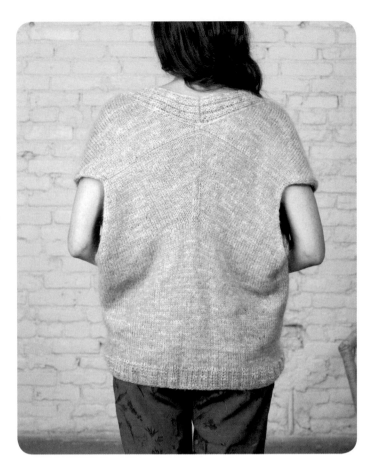

Next Row: [K2, p2] 4 times, k1, sm, M1R, k to last 3 sts, k2tog, sl1 wyib.

Sizes M and L only:
Repeat last 2 rows once more—54 (58, 63, 67, 70, 76) sts rem.

All sizes
Next Row (WS): P to m, sm, p1, [k2, p2] 3 times, k2, sl2 wyif.

Next Row (RS): [K2, p2] 4 times, k1, sm, M1R, k to last 3 sts, k2tog, sl1 wyib.

Repeat last 2 rows a further 24 (25, 27, 28, 30, 31) times—50 (52, 56, 58, 62, 64) rows total.

Transfer the 54 (58, 63, 67, 70, 76) left front sts onto a holder or waste yarn. Break yarn leaving a 6" (15 cm) tail.

BACK
Transfer the 80 (88, 100, 108, 116, 128) back sts to the needles.

With WS facing, attach yarn and work as follows:

Next Row (WS): P to last st, sl1 wyif.

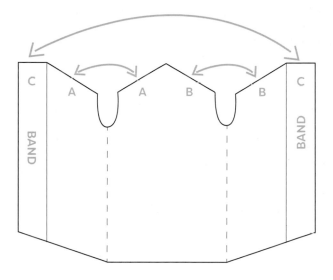

Next Row (RS): Slip the first 2 sts and pass the first st over the second (this counts as first BO), BO 1 (1, 1, 1, 1, 1) st, k to last st, sl1 wyb—2 sts dec'd, 78 (86, 98, 106, 114, 126) sts rem.

Dec Row (WS): Slip the first 2 sts and pass the first st over the second (this counts as first BO), BO 1 (1, 1, 1, 1, 1) st, p to last st, sl1 wyib—2 sts dec'd, 76 (84, 96, 104, 112, 124) sts rem.

Sizes XL and XXL only:
Repeat last 2 rows once more—76 (84, 96, 104, 108, 120) sts rem.

All sizes

Dec Row (RS): Slip the first 2 sts and BO the first st over the second (this counts as first BO), k to last st, sl1 wyib—1 st dec'd, 75 (83, 95, 103, 107, 119) sts rem.

Dec Row (WS): Slip the first 2 sts and BO the first st over the second (this counts as first BO), p to last st, sl1 wyib—1 st dec'd, 74 (82, 94,102, 106, 118) sts rem.

Sizes M and L only:
Repeat last 2 rows once more—74 (82, 92, 100, 106, 118) sts rem.

All sizes:

Set-up Row (RS): K37 (41, 46, 50, 53, 59), pm, k to last st, sl1 wyib—74 (82, 92,100, 106, 118) sts rem.

Next Row (WS): P to last st, sl1 wyif.

Repeat last 2 rows a further 7 (8, 7, 8, 8, 9) times—16 (18, 16, 18, 18, 20) rows total.

UPPER BACK AND SHOULDER SHAPING
Next Row (RS): K1, ssk, k to 1 st before marker, M1L, k1, sm, k1, M1R, k to last 3 sts, k2tog, sl1 wyib.

Next Row (WS): P to last st before end, sl1 wyif.

Repeat last 2 rows a further 14 (15, 15, 16, 17, 18) times—30 (32, 32, 34, 36, 38) rows total.

JOIN SHOULDERS
Transfer the 37 (41, 46, 50, 53, 59) Right Front sts to another needle, leaving the 17 Front Band sts on the holder.

Working on the WS and using the 3-needle BO method, sew together the 37 (41, 46, 50, 53, 59) sts of Right Front and Back sts.

Transfer the 37 (41, 46, 50, 53, 59) Left Front sts to another needle, leaving the 17 Front Band sts on the holder.

Working on the WS and using the 3-needle BO method, sew together the 37 (41, 46, 50, 53, 59) sts of Left Front and Back sts.

JOIN BANDS AT BACK NECK
Transfer the 17 band sts of both bands to 2 different needles.

Working on the WS and using the 3 Needle BO method, sew together 17 sts of each band.

ARMHOLE I-CORD FINISHING
Pick up 82 (86, 92, 96, 102, 106) sts along armholes. Using the Backward Loop CO method, CO 3 sts on the left needle, then work as follows: *K2, ssk, slip these 3 sts back to left-hand needle, repeat from * until last 3 sts on right-hand needle. Cut yarn, leaving a 10" tail, and seam those last 3 sts with the previously CO sts at the beginning.

FINISHING
Weave in ends. Block pieces to measurements.

CYNNES ANKLET SOCKS

lydia gluck

LYDIA GLUCK is the co-founder and editor of *Pom Pom Quarterly* magazine and leads its London office. She was born in London, grew up in Wales, studied in Manchester, and left her heart in Mexico. She has always had a crafty streak, dabbling in everything from furniture making to papier-mâché. Lydia has a background in linguistics and spends a lot of time trying to draw parallels between knitting and grammar.

MATERIALS
2 hanks CoopKnits Socks Yeah! (75% wool, 25% nylon; 231 yd/50 g): #103 Axinite

Size U.S. 1½ (2.5 mm), 40" (100 cm) circular needle for magic loop or set of size U.S. 1½ (2.5 mm) double-pointed needles (dpns)—*or size needed to obtain gauge*

Size U.S. 1 (2.25 mm), 40" (100 cm) circular needle for magic loop or set of size U.S. 1 (2.25 mm) double-pointed needles (dpns)—*or size needed to obtain gauge*

Stitch marker, darning needle, waste yarn, pins

SIZES
S (M, L)

FINISHED MEASUREMENTS
7½ (8¼, 9)" (19 [21, 23] cm) foot circumference

Foot length is adjustable.

GAUGE
32 sts x 44 rnds = 4" (10 cm) in Stockinette Stitch on larger needles, after blocking

NOTES
Cynnes are worked from the toe up. The instructions are written for working magic loop on long circular needles. If using double-pointed needles or a short circular needle, place a marker at the halfway point to distinguish "needle 1" sts from "needle 2."

DIRECTIONS (MAKE 2)

TOE
Using smaller needles and Judy's Magic Cast-On (see page 192), CO 24 (26, 28) sts (12 [13, 14] sts per needle). If you wish, insert a marker to mark start of the round.

Knit 1 round, knitting through the back loop of the stitches on needle 2, which will be twisted from the cast-on.

Begin increasing for the toe.

Rnd 1: Needle (N) 1: kfb, k to last st, kfb; N2: kfb, k to last st, kfb—4 sts increased.

Rnd 2: Knit around.

Rep last 2 rnds 8 (9, 10) more times—60 (66, 72) sts; 30 (33, 36) per needle.

Knit 2 more rounds.

FOOT
Rnd 1: N1: K1, [p1, k2] rep until 2 sts remain, p1, k1; N2: knit.

Rnd 2: Knit around.

Rnds 1 and 2 set up Broken Rib. Rep these 2 rounds until foot measures 4 (4½, 5)" (10 [11.5, 12.5] cm) less than desired length of foot.

GUSSET
Rnd 1: N1: k to end; N2: kfb, k to last 2 sts, kfb, k1—2 sts increased.

Rnd 2: Knit around.

Rep these 2 rounds 11 (12, 14) more times. 54 (59, 66) sts on N2—84 (92, 102) sts total.

TURN HEEL

Knit to end of N1, then work back and forth in rows on N2 only as follows.

Short Row 1 (RS): K41 (45, 51), w&t.

Short Row 2 (WS): P28 (31, 36), w&t.

Short Row 3: K to 1 st before wrapped st, w&t.

Short Row 4: P to 1 st before wrapped st, w&t.

Repeat Short Rows 3 and 4, 6 (7, 8) more times—14 (15, 16) center sts with 8 (9, 10) wrapped sts on each side, plus 12 (13, 15) gusset stitches on each side.

Next Rnd: Knit to end of round, picking up wraps and knitting them together with their sts as you go.

GUSSET

Set-up Rnd: N1: Work Broken Rib; N2: picking up the remaining wraps and knitting them together with their sts through the back loop as you go, k42 (44, 49), ssk, turn.

Row 1 (WS): Sl1 wyif, p28 (29, 32), p2tog. Turn.

Row 2 (RS): Sl1 wyib, k28 (29, 32), ssk. Turn.

Rep Rows 1 and 2, 10 (11, 13) more times. DO NOT TURN on the final row—1 side st rem; 31 (34, 37) sts on N2.

Next Rnd: N1: Work Broken Rib; N2: k2tog to complete the gusset decrease, k to end—30 (33, 36) sts on N2; 60 (66, 72) sts total.

LEG

Begin working Broken Rib over the whole round again as follows:

Rnd 1: N1: K1, [p1, k2] rep until 2 sts remain, p1, k1; N2: knit.

Rnd 2: Knit around.

Rep Rnds 1 and 2 until foot measures measures 1" (2.5 cm) from end of gusset decreases.

Work in Stockinette St (knit all rnds) for an additional 1" (2.5 cm).

PICOT HEM

Next Rnd: *Yo, k2tog; rep from * to end of rnd.

Knit 1 round.

Change to smaller needles and continue to work in Stockinette in the rnd for an additional 1" (2.5 cm).

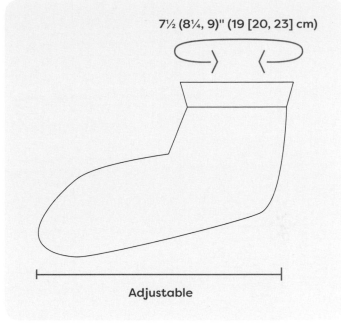

7½ (8¼, 9)" (19 [20, 23] cm)

Adjustable

Work sewn hem as follows:

1. Transfer sts to scrap yarn (you don't have to do this, but you might find it easier).

2. Cut working yarn about 7" (20 cm) longer than the circumference of the sock, and thread onto darning needle.

3. Fold hem into position, securing with blunt pins if desired.

4. Attach your hem to the line of purl bumps above where the sts sit when the hem is folded as follows:

Thread yarn through purl bump corresponding to stitch to be sewn; next, thread yarn through corresponding stitch on needle, drop this stitch off scrap yarn and slide next stitch along ready to be sewn.

Rep Step 4 until all stitches have been sewn.

FINISHING

Weave in ends, hand-wash, and dry flat.

BEHAAGLIJK BRIOCHE COWL

nancy marchant

NANCY MARCHANT, aka the Queen of Brioche, first discovered brioche stitch when she moved to the Netherlands in 1976. She fell in love with brioche knitting and since has written about it for knitting magazines, books, and her own website, which is widely seen as the quintessential modern resource on the subject.

MATERIALS
2 hanks Brooklyn Tweed Vale (100% American Rambouillet wool, 450 yd/100 g): 1 hank each in Parchment (light color, LC) and Heron (dark color, DC)

Size U.S. 4 (3.5mm), 24" (60 cm) circular needle—*or size needed to obtain gauge*

Stitch markers, tapestry needle

FINISHED MEASUREMENTS
Approximately 12½" (32 cm) tall with a 29" (74 cm) circumference

GAUGE
23.5 sts x 22.5 LC and DC rounds = 4" (10 cm) in stitch pattern

PATTERN NOTES
This cowl is worked in the round, in a stitch pattern that is a multiple of 16 sts and 6 rounds.

In two-color brioche, 2 rounds are worked for each counted round that appears on the face of the fabric. To make it easier to count the rounds, count the stitches in the dominant LC knit columns as viewed from the public side.

When changing colors at the beginning of a round, don't cross your threads. At the end of an LC round, pick up DC underneath LC. At the end of a DC round, pick up LC that is sitting across the just-worked stitch and take it to the back to work next round.

SPECIAL STITCHES
brk (brioche knit—also known as a bark) = knit the stitch that was slipped in the previous row together with its yarn-over.

brp (brioche purl—also known as a burp) = purl the stitch that was slipped in the previous row together with its yarn-over.

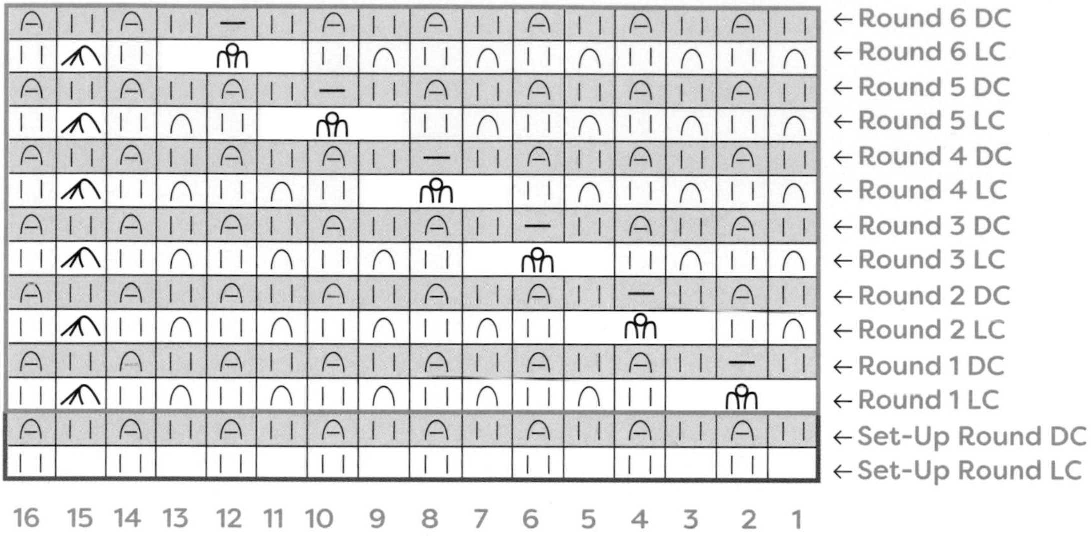

Chart

Rows (top to bottom), read right-to-left over columns 16–1:

- ← Round 6 DC
- ← Round 6 LC
- ← Round 5 DC
- ← Round 5 LC
- ← Round 4 DC
- ← Round 4 LC
- ← Round 3 DC
- ← Round 3 LC
- ← Round 2 DC
- ← Round 2 LC
- ← Round 1 DC
- ← Round 1 LC
- ← Set-Up Round DC
- ← Set-Up Round LC

Column numbers: 16 15 14 13 12 11 10 9 8 7 6 5 4 3 2 1

sl1yo = the action that creates the shawled stitch.

This action works differently for a bark row than for a burp row, but one aspect remains standard: The working yarn must always be in front before slipping the stitch. On a burp row the working yarn is in place before slipping the stitch, but in a bark row you need to first bring the yarn to the front, and then slip the stitch. This slipped stitch, with its yarn-over shawl, is considered one stitch.

sl1yo following a k or brk st = bring the working yarn under the needle to the front of the work, slip the next stitch purlwise, then bring the yarn over the needle (and over the slipped stitch) to the back, in position to work the following stitch.

sl1yo following a p or brp st = the working yarn is already in front. Slip the next stitch purlwise, then bring the yarn over the needle (and over the slipped stitch), and then to the front under the needle, into position to work the following stitch.

brkyobrk (2-stitch increase) = brk1, leaving the stitch on left-hand needle, yarn over (yarn forward under needle, then over needle to back), then brk1 into the same stitch—2 stitches increased. When a brkyobrk increase is used, 3 single stitches bloom out of the center of 1 stitch. These 3 stitches will be worked separately in the following row, since they are not yet shawled.

brLsl dec (2-stitch decrease that slants to the left, involving 3 sts) = slip the first stitch knitwise, brk the following 2 stitches together, pass the slipped stitch over.

Two-Color Long Tail Cast-On

Tie your two yarns together, leaving 6" (15 cm) tails. Wrap the LC around the thumb and the DC around the index finger, work the long tail cast-on just as you would if you were using only one yarn. The tail can be used later on to loosen up the cast-on if it is too tight.

Stem-Stitch Bind-Off

*Insert the needle into the second stitch from front to back and pull the yarn through. Then insert needle in to the first stitch from back to front, going under the horizontal strand just made. Pull the yarn through and drop the first stitch from the knitting needle. Repeat from *. This leaves a bind off with an appearance similar to the two-color long tail cast-on.

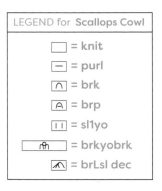

LEGEND for **Scallops Cowl**

☐ = knit

⊟ = purl

⌒ = brk

⌂ = brp

⊞ = sl1yo

⋔ = brkyobrk

⟋⟍ = brLsl dec

Scallops Cowl
CO a multiple of 16 sts.

DIRECTIONS

Using the Two-Color Long Tail Cast-On, CO 176 sts.

Join to begin working in the round, being careful not to twist the cast-on stitches. Remember to drop the first "knot" at beginning of cast-on. Place marker to indicate beginning of rnd.

Set-Up Rnd (LC): *k1, sl1yo; rep from * around, dropping yarn to front at end of rnd.

Set-Up Rnd DC: *sl1yo, brp1; rep from * around, dropping yarn to front at end of rnd.

Rnd 1 (LC): *brkyobrk, sl1yo, [brk1, sl1yo] 5 times, brLsl dec, sl1yo; rep from * around.

Rnd 1 (DC): *sl1yo, p1, [sl1yo, brp1] 7 times; rep from * around.

Rnd 2 (LC): *brk1, sl1yo, brkyobrk, sl1yo, [brk1, sl1yo] 4 times, brLsl dec, sl1yo; rep from * around.

Rnd 2 (DC): *sl1yo, brp1, sl1yo, p1, [sl1yo, brp1] 6 times; rep from * around.

Rnd 3 (LC): *[brk1, sl1yo] twice, brkyobrk, sl1yo, [brk1, sl1yo] 3 times, brLsl dec, sl1yo; rep from * around.

Rnd 3 (DC): *[sl1yo, brp1] twice, sl1yo, p1, [sl1yo, brp1] 5 times; rep from * around.

Rnd 4 (LC): *[brk1, sl1yo] 3 times, brkyobrk, sl1yo, [brk1, sl1yo] twice, brLsl dec, sl1yo; rep from * around.

Rnd 4 (DC): *[sl1yo, brp1] 3 times, sl1yo, p1, [sl1yo, brp1] 4 times; rep from * around.

Rnd 5 (LC): *[brk1, sl1yo] 4 times, brkyobrk, sl1yo, brk1, sl1yo, brLsl dec, sl1yo; rep from * around.

Rnd 5 (DC): *[sl1yo, brp1] 4 times, sl1yo, p1, [sl1yo, brp1] 3 times; rep from * around.

Rnd 6 (LC): *[brk1, sl1yo] 5 times, brkyobrk, sl1yo, brLsl dec, sl1yo; rep from * around.

Rnd 6 (DC): *[sl1yo, brp1] 5 times, sl1yo, p1, [sl1yo, brp1] twice; rep from * around.

Rnds 1–6 constitute the pattern. Repeat these rounds until cowl is desired height (12 pattern repeats worked in sample), ending with a Round 6 LC.

Last Rnd 6 (DC): *[k1, brp1] 5 times, k1, p1, [k1, brp1] twice; rep from * around.

Cut DC and weave in end. Cut LC 3 times longer than the circumference of the cowl. Using the Stem Stitch Bind-Off, BO loosely. After binding off 10–15 stitches, go back and pull up and tighten the loose bind-off stitches just made so that it matches your cast-on. Then continue with your bind off to the end.

Work in ends and block as desired.

TASCHE BOHO BAG

drew emborsky, aka the crochet dude

DREW EMBORSKY, aka the Crochet Dude, is a crochet designer, instructor, author, and personality. He was the crochet expert on four seasons of PBS's *Knit & Crochet Now,* developed a signature line of hooks and tools for major craft stores nationwide, and travels the country to impart his crochet knowledge to students of all levels.

MATERIALS
2 hanks Be So Tender by Kristin Omdahl (100% certified organic cotton; 100g/140 yds): Cloud

Size U.S. J-10 (6 mm) crochet hook

Tooled leather strap by Allred Leather Company, coordinating fabric for lining (optional)

FINISHED MEASUREMENTS
14" (35.5 cm) wide at the bottom x 12" (30.5 cm) tall (without fringe or strap)

GAUGE
Not critical for this project

NOTES
First the front of the purse is crocheted, then it is turned over and you work the back of the purse, working into the original foundation chain; sides are then seamed. The flap is worked separately then whipstitched on.

FRONT OF PURSE
Row 1 (WS): Ch 51, 2 dc in 7th ch from hook, ch 2, 2 dc in next ch, sk 2 ch, *dc in next 2 ch, sk 2 ch, 2 dc in next ch, ch 2, 2 dc in next ch, sk 2, rep from * across, end with 1 dc in last ch, turn.

Row 2 (RS): Ch 3, *(2 dc, ch 2, 2 dc) in ch 2 sp, sk 2 dc, fpdc around next 2 sts, rep from * across, end with (2 dc, ch 2, 2 dc) in ch 2 sp, sk 2 dc, dc in top of turning ch, turn.

Row 3: Ch 3, *(2 dc, ch 2, 2 dc) in ch 2 sp, sk 2 dc, bpdc around next 2 sts, rep from * across, end with (2 dc, ch 2, 2 dc) in ch 2 sp, sk 2 dc, dc in top of turning ch, turn.

Rows 4–9: Rep Rows 2 and 3.

Row 10: Rep Row 2.

Row 11: Ch 3, *(2 dc, ch 2, 2 dc) in ch 2 sp, sk 2 dc, bpdc2tog around next 2 sts, rep from * across, end with (2 dc, ch 2, 2 dc) in ch 2 sp, sk 2 dc, dc in top of turning ch, turn.

Row 12: Ch 3, *(2 dc, ch 2, 2 dc) in ch 2 sp, sk 2 dc, fpdc around next st, rep from * across, end with (2 dc, ch 2, 2 dc) in ch 2 sp, sk 2 dc, dc in top of turning ch, turn.

Row 13: Ch 3, *(2 dc, ch 2, 2 dc) in ch 2 sp, sk 2 dc, bpdc around next st, rep from * across, end with (2 dc, ch 2, 2 dc) in ch 2 sp, sk 2 dc, dc in top of turning ch, turn

Row 14: Rep Row 12.

Row 15: Ch 3, *(dc, ch 2, dc) in ch 2 sp, sk 2 dc, bpdc around next st, rep from * across, end with (dc, ch 2, dc) in ch 2 sp, sk 2 dc, dc in top of turning ch, turn.

Row 16: Ch 3, *(dc, ch 2, dc) in ch 2 sp, sk 1 dc, bpdc around next st, rep from * across, end with (dc, ch 2, dc) in ch 2 sp, sk 1 dc, dc in top of turning ch, turn.

Row 17: Ch 3, *(dc, ch 2, dc) in ch 2 sp, sk 1 dc, bpdc around next st, rep from * across, end with (dc, ch 2, dc) in ch 2 sp, sk 1 dc, dc in top of turning ch, turn.

Fasten off.

BACK OF PURSE
With WS facing, turn project over and working in the original foundation row, attach yarn with a slip st to bottom of first st:

Row 1: Ch 3, sk 2 ch, 2 dc in next ch (this should correspond to the 2 dc from the first row of the front of the purse, creating a mirror image), ch 2, 2 dc in next ch, sk 2 ch, *dc in next 2 ch, sk 2 ch, 2 dc in next ch, ch 2, 2 dc in next ch, sk 2, rep from * across, end with 1 dc in last ch, turn.

Rows 2–17: Repeat as for front of purse.

FLAP

Row 1: Ch 4, 8 dc in 4th ch from hook, turn.

Row 2 (RS): Ch 3, *fpdc around next st, (dc, ch 2, dc) in next st, rep from * across, ending with dc in last st, turn.

Row 3: Ch 3, *bpdc around next st, (2dc, ch 2, 2dc) in next st, rep from * across, ending with dc in last st, turn.

Row 4: Ch 3, *fpdc around next st, (2dc, ch 3, 2dc) in next st, rep from * across, ending with dc in last st, turn.

Row 5: Ch 3, *bpdc around next st, (2dc, ch 2, 2dc, ch 2, 2 dc) in next st, rep from * across, ending with dc in last st, turn.

Row 6: Ch 3, *fpdc around next st, (2dc, ch 3, 2dc) in next 2 ch-2 spaces, rep from * across, ending with dc in last st, turn.

Fasten off.

FINISHING

Fold purse in half at the foundation row with RS facing each other, whipstitch the side seams.

Line up flap with back side of purse opening and with RS facing each other, whipstitch seam.

For tassels, cut yarn in 17" (43 cm) lengths, fold each in half to create a loop, pull that loop through the project where desired, then pull the cut ends through that loop and pull tight. Attach tassels evenly along bottom and along bottom edge of flap.

ATTACH STRAP
Tabs (make 2):

Ch 7.

Row 1: Dc in 4th ch from hook, dc in next 3 chs. Turn.

Row 2: Ch 3, dc in each dc. Turn.

Repeat Row 2 until tab measure 3" (1.5 cm). Fasten off.

Insert a tab into each metal loop of strap. Attach each tab to each side of purse where flap begins.

Weave in all ends.

Optional: Line with coordinating fabric if desired.

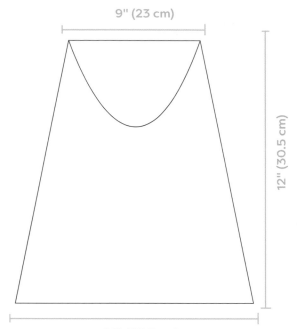

9" (23 cm)

12" (30.5 cm)

14" (35.5 cm)

TEAS
FAIR ISLE
SNOOD

tanis gray

TANIS GRAY is a graduate of RISD and lives in Fairfax, Virginia, with her mechanical engineer husband and two children. She has been in the creative field for many years, including roles at Martha Stewart, HBO, Focus Features, Hungryman Productions, and as the yarn editor at *Vogue Knitting* and Sixth & Spring and co-editor of *Knit.1.* Tanis teaches, has over 450 published knitting designs, was a featured cast member on *Knitting Daily* with Vickie Howell (PBS), and has multiple online classes, focused on Fair Isle, on Craftsy. She has won the American Heritage Award and the National Women in the Arts Award numerous times for Fiber Arts.

MATERIALS
2 hanks Neighborhood Fiber Co. Studio Worsted (100% superwash merino wool, 400 yd/227 g skein): 1 hank Edgewood (dark green, A), 1 hank Canton (turquoise, B)

Size U.S. 6 (4 mm), 32" (80 cm) circular needle—*or size needed to obtain gauge*

Size U.S. 8 (5 mm), 32" (80 cm) circular needle—*or size needed to obtain gauge*

Stitch marker, tapestry needle

FINISHED MEASUREMENTS
52" (132 cm) circumference at widest point x 20" (51 cm) height

GAUGE
18 sts x 21 rnds = 4" (10 cm) in colorwork chart pattern on larger needles, after blocking

NOTES
Teas Fair Isle Snood is worked in the round from the bottom up. The German Twisted Cast-On (see page 190) is recommended for a stretchy cast-on edge. The colorwork body is worked from a chart in three sections, with a decrease round between each section for a tapered silhouette. While working the colorwork pattern, be careful to maintain color dominance consistently throughout the cowl.

BOTTOM HEM

Using smaller needles, with A and the German Twisted Cast-On technique (page 190), CO 216 sts and join into round, being careful not to twist. Pm indicating beg of rnd.

Work in Garter Stitch (knit 1 rnd, purl 1 rnd) for a total of 8 rnds.

BODY

BEGIN WORKING FROM CHART

Change to larger needles, join B, and work rnds 1–46 of chart once, repeating each chart row 9 times across the rnd.

Rnd 47: With A, [k7, k2tog] across rnd—192 sts.

Continue chart, working rnds 48–74 once. You will now repeat each chart row 8 times across the rnd.

Rnd 75: With B, [k6, k2tog] across rnd—168 sts.

Continue chart, working rnds 76–97 once. You will now repeat each chart row 8 times across the rnd.

TOP HEM

Break A. Continue working with B only.

Change to smaller needles and work in Garter Stitch (knit 1 rnd, purl 1 rnd) for 6 rnds.

Knit 1 rnd.

BO all stitches purlwise.

FINISHING

Weave in all loose ends with tapestry needle. Soak in cool water and wool wash and block to measurements.

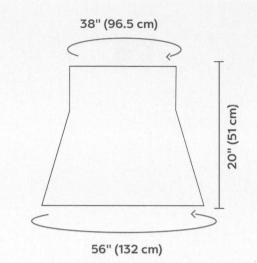

38" (96.5 cm)

20" (51 cm)

56" (132 cm)

LEGEND for
Teas Fair Isle Snood

◼ = knit in color A

☐ = knit in color B

| = decrease
rounds;
see written
instructions

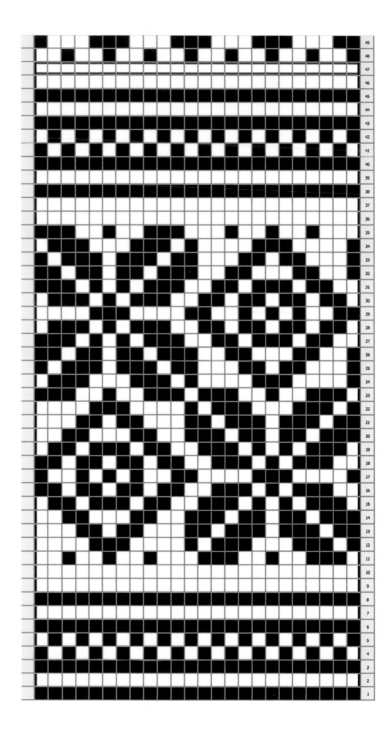

CHALEUR CABLED HAT

kate gagnon osborn

KATE GAGNON OSBORN
is the co-founder (along with Courtney Kelley) of Kelbourne Woolens, a North American distributor of excellent knitting and crochet yarns, creator of distinctive educational patterns, developer of useful notions and accessories, and educator in the industry.

MATERIALS
1 hank Kelbourne Woolens Scout (100% wool; 274 yd/100 g): Orchid Heather

Size U.S. 3 (3.25 mm), 16" (40 cm) circular needle—*or size needed to obtain gauge*

Size U.S. 6 (4 mm), 16" (40 cm) circular needle—*or size needed to obtain gauge*

Set of size U.S. 6 (4 mm) double-pointed needles (dpns)

Stitch marker, tapestry needle, cable needle (cn)

FINISHED MEASUREMENTS
16½" (42 cm) circumference, unstretched. 10¼" (26 cm) height, brim folded

GAUGE
29 sts x 30 rnds = 4" (10 cm) in K1, P Ribbing, unstretched, on smaller needles, after blocking

2 Cable Chart, unstretched, (24 sts) = 3" (7.5 cm) on larger needles, after blocking

PATTERN NOTES
Chaleur is worked in the round from the bottom up. After the ribbing is complete, the body is worked from a chart in an all-over cable pattern. Increases are incorporated into the first two rounds of the chart to accommodate the cable gauge. When working from the chart, work the stitches outside the repeat once, and then the stitches inside the repeat 10 times around.

Work brim and body on circular needles, changing to double-pointed needles on the crown when necessary.

The brim and body pattern are both quite stretchy and the hat is designed to fit an average adult woman's head.

SPECIAL STITCHES
C1/1R: Sl 1 st to cn, hold back, k1; k1 from cn

C2/2R: Sl 2 sts to cn, hold back, k2; k2 from cn

C2/2RP: Sl 2 sts to cn, hold back, k2; p2 from cn

C1/2RP: Sl 1 st to cn, hold back, k2; p1 from cn

C2/2L: Sl 2 sts to cn, hold front, k2; k2 from cn

C2/1L: Sl 2 sts to cn, hold front, k1; k2 from cn

C2/1Linc: Sl 2 sts to cn, hold front, k1f+b; k2 from cn—1 st increased

C2/2Ldec: Sl 2 sts to cn, hold front, k2tog, k1; k2 from cn—1 st decreased

C2/2LP: Sl 2 sts to cn, hold front, p2; k2 from cn

C2/1LP: Sl 2 sts to cn, hold front, p1; k2 from cn

DIRECTIONS

BRIM

Using smaller circular needle, CO 110 sts. Join for working in the rnd, being careful not to twist sts. Pm indicating beg of rnd.

Next Rnd: *K1, p1; rep from * around. 1x1 rib established. Work in 1x1 rib for 4¾" (12 cm). Change to larger circular needle.

BODY

SET-UP FOR CHART

Set-up Rnd: *P2, k1, p2, k5; rep from * around.

BEGIN WORKING FROM CHART

Work Rnds 1–46 of Cable Chart—121 sts after working Rnd 1, 132 sts after working Rnd 2, and 88 sts after working Rnd 46. Remove all markers except for end-of-rnd marker.

CROWN

Rnd 1: Remove marker, *C2/2R, p1, C1/1R, p1; rep from * to 7 sts rem, C2/2R, p1, C1/1R, replace marker. (Last st of rnd is now first st of next rnd.)

Rnd 2: *C1/2RP, (sl 2 sts to cn, hold front, p1; k2 from cn), k2; rep from * around.

Rnd 3: *K2, p2tog, C2/2L; rep from * around—77 sts.

Rnd 4: K2, *p1, k6; rep from * to 5 sts rem, p1, k4, remove marker, k2, replace marker.

Rnd 5: *P1, k2tog, C2/2R; rep from * around—66 sts.

Rnd 6: *P1, k3, k2tog; rep from * around—55 sts.

Rnd 7: *P1, C2/2LDec; rep from * around—44 sts.

Rnd 8: *P1, k1, k2tog; rep from * around—33 sts.

Rnd 9: *K3tog; rep from * around—11 sts.

FINISHING

Cut yarn, leaving an 8" (20 cm) tail. Thread through live sts. Pull tight to close hole at top of hat, fasten off, and weave in ends. Soak in cool water and wool wash and block to measurements.

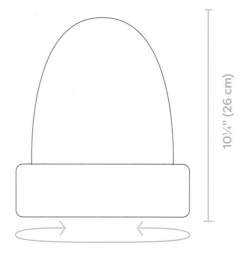

10¼" (26 cm)

16½" (42 cm)

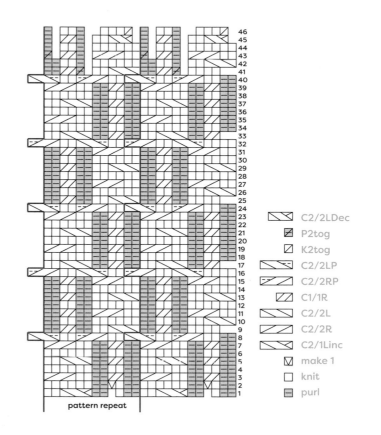

C2/2LDec	
P2tog	
K2tog	
C2/2LP	
C2/2RP	
C1/1R	
C2/2L	
C2/2R	
C2/1Linc	
make 1	
knit	
purl	

pattern repeat

WÄRME MITTS

heather walpole

HEATHER WALPOLE
is the owner and face
of Ewe Ewe Yarns. Her
background as a graphic
designer and designer for
Ikea translates into the
fresh color choices of EEY's
palettes and the clean,
modular aesthetics of her
knit and crochet designs.

MATERIALS
4 balls Ewe Ewe Yarns
Wooly Worsted (100%
merino wool, 95 yd/50 g):
1 ball each in #30 Saffron
(A), #70 Aquamarine (B),
#05 Cotton Candy (C),
and #97 Brushed Silver (D)

Set of size U.S. 7 (4.5 mm)
double-pointed needles
(dpns)—*or size needed to
obtain gauge*

Tapestry needle

FINISHED MEASUREMENTS
8" (20 cm) circumference,
unstretched. 6½"
(16.5 cm) height

SIZE
Pattern is written for one
size, approx. a women's
large. Consider using
a smaller needle size to
make a slightly smaller
mitt or a larger needle size
to create a larger mitt.

GAUGE
18 sts x 40 rows = 4"
(10 cm) in garter stitch

PATTERN NOTES
Each mitt starts with a
small center panel and is
worked back and forth.
The project is then rotated
clockwise and new stitches
are picked up to create
each adjoining panel.
Although the mitts are
worked back and forth,
double-pointed needles
are recommended for ease
of working a few stitches
at a time.

DIRECTIONS

RIGHT HAND MITT

BOX 1:
Using color A, cast on 5 sts.

Knit 18 rows.

BO all sts on an RS row,
leaving the last stitch on
the needle.

BOX 2:
With RS still facing, rotate
your work 90 degrees
clockwise.

With color B, PU 10 sts along
the long edge of Box 1.

Row 1 (WS): K to last 2 sts,
k2tog.

Knit 9 rows. BO all sts on
an RS row, leaving the
last stitch on the needle.

BOX 3:
With RS facing, rotate your
work 90 degrees clockwise.

With color C, PU 5 sts along
the short edge of Box 2,
and 5 sts along the cast-on
edge of Box 1. Work as for
Box 2, beginning with Row 1.

BOX 4:
With RS facing, rotate your
work 90 degrees clockwise.

With color B, PU 5 sts along
the cast-on edge of Box 3
and 10 sts along the long
edge of Box 1—16 sts.

Work as for Box 2,
beginning with Row 1.

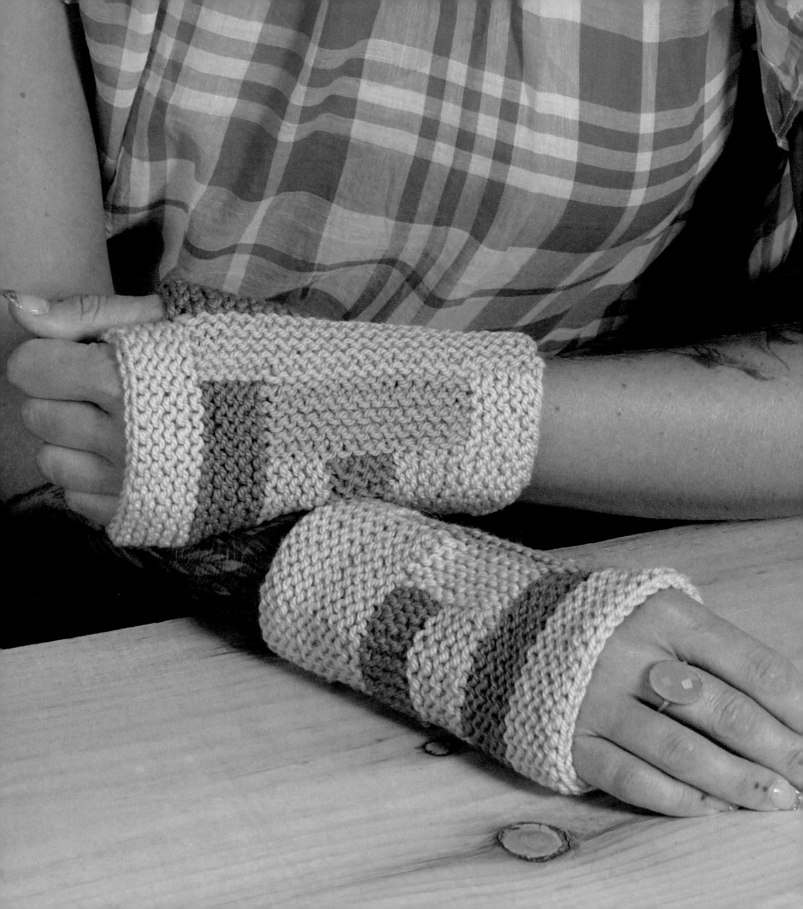

BOX 5:

With RS facing, rotate your work 90 degrees clockwise.

With color D, PU 5 sts along the short edge of Box 4, 5 sts along the bind-off edge of Box 1, and 5 sts along the short edge of Box 2—16 sts.

Work as for Box 2, beginning with Row 1.

BOX 6:

With RS facing, rotate your work 90 degrees clockwise.

With color A, PU 5 sts along the short edge of Box 5, 10 sts along the bind-off edge of Box 2, and 5 sts along the short edge of Box 3—21 sts.

Work as for Box 2, beginning with Row 1.

BOX 7:

With RS facing, rotate your work 90 degrees clockwise.

With color D, PU 5 sts along the short edge of Box 6, 10 sts along the bind-off edge of Box 3, and 5 sts along the short edge of Box 4—21 sts.

Work as for Box 2, beginning with Row 1.

BOX 8:

With RS facing, rotate your work 90 degrees clockwise.

With color C, PU 5 sts along the short edge of Box 7, 15 sts along the bind-off edge of Box 4, and 5 sts along the short edge of Box 5—26 sts.

Work as for Box 2, beginning with Row 1.

BOX 9:

With RS facing, rotate your work 90 degrees clockwise.

With color B, PU 5 sts along the short edge of Box 8, 15 sts along the bind-off edge of Box 5, and 5 sts along the short edge of Box 6—26 sts.

Work as for Box 2, beginning with Row 1.

BOX 10:

With RS facing, rotate your work 90 degrees clockwise.

With color C, PU 5 sts along the short edge of Box 9, 20 sts along the bind-off edge of Box 6, and 5 sts along the short edge of Box 7—31 sts.

Work as for Box 2, beginning with Row 1.

RIGHT THUMB GUSSET

With RS facing, rotate your work 90 degrees clockwise.

With color A, PU 10 sts along short edge of Box 10, 20 sts along bind-off edge of Box 7, and 5 sts along short edge of Box 8—31 sts.

Cast on 3 sts using the backward loop method. Turn.

Row 1 (WS): K2, k2tog. Turn.

Row 2 (RS): K3.

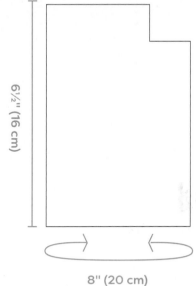

6½" (16 cm)

8" (20 cm)

Repeat Rows 1 and 2, seven more times. There should be 23 picked-up sts and 3 gusset sts remaining.

Row 3 (WS): K2, k2tog. Turn.

Row 4 (RS): K1, kfb, k1—4 sts.

Row 5: K3, k2tog. Turn.

Row 6: K4.

Row 7 (WS): K4. Turn.

Row 8 (RS): K to last 2 sts, kfb, k1—1 gusset st increased.

Row 9: K5. Turn.

Row 10: K4, k2tog—1 picked-up st decreased.

Continue working as for Rows 7–10 six more times, increasing one gusset st and decreasing 2 picked-up sts on each repeat. There should be 11 gusset sts on the left needle, and 7 picked-up sts remain.

THUMB HOLE

Next Row (WS): BO 9 sts, k2tog, BO 1 more st. All gusset sts are now bound off.

Cast on 3 sts using the backward loop method. Do not turn; continue to work across the 7 picked-up sts that remain at the top of the mitt.

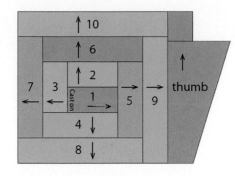

left hand mitt

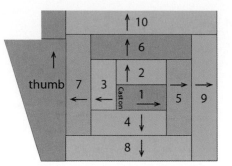

right hand mitt

Next row (WS): K2, k2tog. Turn.

Next row (RS): K3. Turn.

Continue working as for the previous 2 rows until 4 sts remain, ending after an RS row.

Next row (WS): K2, k3tog. Turn.

BO all sts. Break yarn leaving a 12" (30.5 cm) tail.

Sew the left edge of the thumb gusset to the right edge of the log cabin square along Boxes 9 and 10, leaving the thumb hole open.

LEFT HAND MITT
Work as for Right Hand Mitt until Thumb Gusset.

LEFT THUMB GUSSET
With RS facing, rotate your work 90 degrees *counterclockwise*.

With color A, PU 25 sts along bind-off edge of Box 9, and 5 sts along short edge of Box 6—31 sts.

Break yarn and rejoin at opposite end. With WS facing, cast on 3 sts using the backward loop method. Turn.

Row 1 (RS): K2, k2tog. Turn.

Row 2 (WS): K3.

Repeat Rows 1 and 2, seven more times. There should be 22 picked-up sts and 3 gusset sts remaining.

Row 3 (RS): K2, k2tog. Turn.

Row 4 (WS): K1, kfb, k1—4 sts.

Row 5: K3, k2tog. Turn.

Row 6: K4.

Row 7 (RS): K3, k2tog. Turn.

Row 8 (WS): K to last 2 sts, kfb, k1—1 st increased.

Row 9: K4, k2tog. Turn.

Row 10: K5.

Continue working as for Rows 7–10 six more times, increasing 1 gusset st and decreasing 2 picked-up sts on each repeat. There should be 11 gusset sts on the left needle, and 6 picked-up sts remain.

THUMB HOLE
Next Row (RS): BO 9 sts, k2tog, BO 1 more st. All gusset sts are now bound off. Turn.

Cast on 2 sts using the backward loop method. Do not turn; continue to work across the 6 picked up sts that remain at the top of the mitt.

Next row (WS): K3. Turn.

Next row (RS): K2, k2tog. Turn.

Continue working as for the previous 2 rows until 3 sts remain, ending after an RS row.

BO all sts. Break yarn, leaving a 12" tail.

FINISHING
Weave in all yarn ends. Block lightly to set the stitches.

CALOR CHEVRON SHAWL

marly bird

MARLY BIRD is a wife, mom, knitting and crochet instructor and designer, podcast host, and national spokesperson for Red Heart Yarns. She has been published in many books and magazines, has a mélange of CreativeBug online classes in her repertoire, and continues to take the yarn industry by storm, most recently through her co-branded Chic Sheep line of yarn in partnership with Red Heart.

MATERIALS
10 balls Red Heart® Chic Sheep by Marly Bird™ (100% merino wool; 187 yds/100g): 2 balls each #5635 Crème de Mint (A), #5641 Sterling (B), #5327 Mai Tai (C), #5632 Polo (D), and #5620 Green Tea (E)

Susan Bates® Hook: Size U.S. I (5.5 mm)—*or size needed to obtain gauge*

Susan Bates® split-lock stitch markers

Susan Bates® Bent Tip Needles

Susan Bates® Tassel and Pom-pom Maker

FINISHED MEASUREMENTS
Wrap 22" (56 cm) x 90" (229 cm)

GAUGE
2 stitch pattern repeats = 10" (25 cm)

PATTERN NOTES
Pattern is customizable to any size. To make the wrap larger or smaller, add or subtract rows to your desired length. To make the wrap longer or shorter, add or subtract chains in the beginning in a multiple of 16. Any change made to the original pattern will also change the yarn amount needed.

COLOR SEQUENCE

3 A	10 A
2 B	2 D
6 C	6 B
2 D	6 D
6 B	6 A
6 E	2 E
2 C	2 B
6 D	6 D
10 B	6 C
6 A	6 B
10 C	2 A
10 E	6 E
6 A	10 D
2 C	6 C
2 E	6 E
	1 row of Double Crochet

Note: This pattern is written in U.S. terms. See page 205 for U.K. conversion chart.

With color A, ch 82.

Row 1: Hdc in 3rd ch from hook and each ch across, turn—80 hdc.

Follow the color sequence for the remainder of instructions.

Row 2: Ch 3 (counts as dc throughout), dc in next st, *[sk next st, dc in next st] twice, dc in ea of next 3 st, 5 dc in next st (counts as a shell), dc in ea of next 4 sts, [sk 1 st, dc in next st] twice; rep from * across, dc in last st, turn—11 shells.

Row 3: Ch 1, sc in ea dc across, turn.

Row 4: Ch 3, dc in next sc, *[sk 1 sc, dc in next sc] twice, [ch 1, sk 1 sc, dc in next sc] twice, [ch 1, dc] twice in prev sc, [ch 1, sk 1 sc, dc in next sc] twice, [sk 1 sc, dc in next sc] twice; rep from * across, dc in last sc, turn.

Row 5: Ch 1, sc in ea dc and ch-1 sp across, turn.

Row 6: Ch 3, dc in next sc, *[sk 1 sc, dc in next sc] twice, dc in ea of next 3 sc, 5 dc in next sc, dc in ea of next 4 sc, [sk 1 sc, dc in next sc] twice; rep from * across, dc in last sc, turn.

Rows 7–162: Rep rows 3–6.

Last row: With color E, ch 3, dc in ea dc across.

Fasten off.

FINISHING

Weave in all ends.

Make 4 tassels with sixty 12½" (32 cm) lengths each. When folded in half the finished tassel will be approx. 6" (15 cm). Apply to corners of shawl.

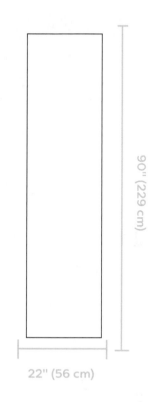

90" (229 cm)

22" (56 cm)

HYGGE TRIANGLE WRAP

vickie howell

MATERIALS

3 hanks Knit Collage Sister (100% wool; 100 yd/250 g): Soft Grey Heather (A)

1 hank Knit Collage Swirl (99% wool, 1% poly sparkle; 60 yd/100 g): Peachy Sparkle (B)

Size 12 mm crochet hook

Locking stitch marker (optional), large-eye tapestry needle

FINISHED MEASUREMENTS

Approx. 72" (183 cm) wide, 34" (86 cm) deep at center

GAUGE

Approx 4 hdc x 6 rows = 4" (10 cm) in yarn A

PATTERN NOTES

This wrap is worked from the top-center out.

SPECIAL STITCHES

MB: make bobble

Note: This pattern is written in U.S. terms. See page 205 for U.K. conversion chart.

DIRECTIONS

BODY

With yarn A, ch 4.

Row 1: [(Hdc, ch 1) 3 times, hdc] in 4th ch from hook (skipped ch3 counts as first hdc and ch-1 sp), turn—5 hdc, 4 ch-1 sps.

Row 2: Ch 4 (counts as dc and ch-1), dc in first st, ch 1, sk next ch, dc in next st, ch 1, sk next ch, (dc, ch 1) 3 times in center hdc, sk next ch, dc in next st, ch 1, sk next ch, (dc, ch 1, dc) in last st, turn—9 dc, 8 ch-1 sps.

Row 3: Ch 3 (counts as hdc and ch-1), hdc in first st, ch 1, sk next ch, *hdc in next st, ch 1, sk next ch**; rep from * to ** across to center st, (hdc, ch 1) 3 times in center st; rep from * to ** to last st, (hdc, ch 1, hdc) in last st, turn—13 hdc, 12 ch-1 sps.

Row 4: Ch 4, dc in first st, ch 1, sk next ch, *dc in next hdc, ch 1, sk next ch **; rep from * to ** across to center st, (dc, ch 1) 3 times in center st, sk next ch; rep from * to ** to last st, (dc, ch 1, dc) in last st, turn—17 dc, 16 ch-1 sps.

Row 5: Rep Row 3—21 hdc, 20 ch-1 sps.

Row 6: Ch 5 (counts as tr and ch-1), tr in first st, ch 1, sk next ch, *tr in next st, ch 1, sk next ch**; rep from * to ** across to center st, (tr, ch 1) 3 times in center st, sk next ch; rep from * to ** to last st, (tr, ch 1, tr) in last st, turn – 25 tr, 24 ch-1 sps.

Cut yarn A; join yarn B.

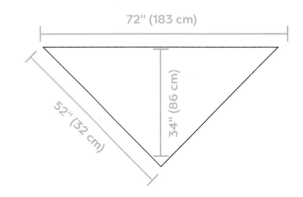

72" (183 cm)

52" (32 cm)

34" (86 cm)

Row 7: Ch 4, dc in first st, ch 1, sk next st, *MB, ch 1, sk 1**; rep from * to ** across to center st, (dc, ch 1) 3 times in center st, sk next ch; rep from * to ** to last st, (dc, ch 1, dc) in last st, turn.

Row 8: Rep Row 3.

Cut yarn B; join yarn A.

Rows 9 and 10: Rep Rows 7 and 8.

Cut yarn A; join yarn B.

Rows 11 and 12: Rep Row 3.

Cut yarn B; join yarn A.

Row 13: Ch 5, tr in first st, ch 1, sk next ch, *tr in next st, ch 1, sk next ch**; rep from * to ** across to center st, (tr, ch 1) 3 times in center st, sk next ch; rep from * to ** to last st, (tr, ch 1, tr) in last st, turn.

Row 14: Ch 3, hdc in first st, ch 1, sk next ch, *hdc in next st, ch 1, sk next ch**; rep from * to ** across to center st, (hdc, ch 1) 3 times in center st, sk next ch, rep from * to ** to last st, (hdc, ch 1, hdc) in last st, turn.

Rows 15–20: Rep Rows 13 and 14.

Fasten off.

MESSY BRAID FRINGE
Using yarn A, cut three 24" (61 cm) strands of yarn. Holding strands together, fold in half. Working into the corner ch-sp, insert crochet hook through RS of shawl edge; lay yarn at the folded point over the hook. Pull yarn through, from back to front, just enough to create loop. Set aside hook and use hands to fold the loop over the edge of the project, pulling the ends of the yarn through the loop. Pull tight-ish.

You'll now have 6 strands hanging (3 strands folded). Separate into 3 groups of 2 strands; loosely braid halfway down fringe and pull to make messy. Use one strand to wrap and tie off braid. Trim and fray ends.

Repeat process, attaching a total of 29 fringe bunches evenly (every 3rd ch-sp gap) across shawl edge.

FINISHING
Weave in ends.

GARAM MUKLUKS

amy small

AMY SMALL is the owner of Knit Collage, a company that specializes in handspun, chunky yarns. Amy began her career as a designer for Free People, an adventure that introduced her to, among other things, the gorgeousness of Indian textiles and culture. She combined her love for hand-spinning with her eye for free-spirited beauty to create an unparalleled brand of artisanal yarns. Read about the co-op of women who spin her company's uniquely gorgeous yarns in the "Community" section of this book, page 50.

MATERIALS

1 (1, 2) hank(s) Knit Collage Sister Yarn (100% wool; 100 yd/215 g skein): Dusty Pink (MC)

1 skein Knit Collage Wildflower Yarn (100% cotton printed fabric, bulky weight; 60 yd/70 g skein): Beatnik (CC)

Size U.S. 15 (10 mm) double-pointed needles (dpns) or long circular needle for magic loop

Size U.S. 15 (10 mm) straight needles

Leather Mukluk slipper sole, 9 (11, 13)" (23 [28, 33] cm) long

Clover mini pom-pom maker (optional)

Tapestry needle, scrap yarn, stitch marker

Scrap yarn for holding stitches

Stitch marker

SIZES
XS/S (M, L) To fit women's shoe sizes 6–7 (8–10, 11–12)

GAUGE
Not critical for this project

PATTERN NOTES
These mukluks are knit from the top down. You'll start off knitting in the round, then divide stitches for the top, front of your slipper, and the back heel portion. Then you'll knit the top portion of your slipper, picking up stitches along the heel flap edge as you go. From then on, you'll only knit the top of the slipper. There will be no knit bottom, because the bottom of your slipper will be the leather sole. At the very end you'll stitch your slipper to the leather bottom. Last, add your i-cord drawstring and tassel and pom-pom embellishments for maximum pretty!

YARN OPTION
Wildflower Yarn was used for the whipstitching and pom-poms/tassels, BUT you can use stash yarn or embroidery floss instead.

DIRECTIONS

With Sister Yarn and double-pointed needles, cast on 24 (28, 32) sts, place marker (pm) and join to knit in the rnd.

Rnds 1–4: *K1, p1; rep from * around.

Continue in Stockinette Stitch (knit every rnd) until your piece measures 7 (8, 9)" (10 [20, 23] cm) long.

HEEL
Divide stitches and knit the top of your slipper and back heel separately. Place 12 (14, 16) sts onto waste yarn and set aside. These will be the stitches that form the top of your slipper.

Rows 1–3: With the 12 (14, 16) sts remaining on the needle for the back heel, continue knitting back and forth in Stockinette St (k on RS, p on WS) for 3 rows, slipping the first st on every row and purling last st. Bind off all sts.

TOP OF SLIPPER

Place live stitches from the waste yarn back onto your needles.

Row 4: With the right side of your work facing you, pick up the 3 sts along the heel flap edge, starting at the outer edge. Knit across the 12 (14, 16) top sts and pick up the final 3 heel flap sts. You will have 18 (20, 22) sts.

Row 5: Purl.

Row 6: K3, ssk, k to last 5 sts, k2tog, k3—16 (18, 20) sts.

Row 7: Purl.

Rep Rows 6 and 7, 2 (3, 4) more times—12 sts.

Continue in Stockinette st for 5 (6, 7)" (12.5 [15, 18] cm) from where you picked up sts.

SHAPE TOE:
Row 1 (RS): K1, ssk, k to last 3 sts, k2tog,

k1—2 sts dec'd.

Row 2 (WS): Purl.

Repeat Rows 1 and 2 three more times—4 sts.

Break yarn and draw it through the remaining 4 sts to cinch close. Weave in your ends and block your slippers lightly with a spray bottle. It is recommended not to completely submerge your slipper in water as this yarn takes a long time to dry.

FINISHING

To attach your slipper to the leather sole, use CC yarn cut in half to make it a little bit skinnier and easier to pass through the tiny slipper-weaving holes. With your darning needle, start at center back and use a whipstitch to stitch your two pieces together. Continue along the entire edge of the slipper sole until the knit portion of your slipper is completely attached to the sole. Repeat for the second side.

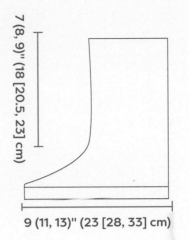

7 (8, 9)" (18 [20.5, 23] cm)

9 (11, 13)" (23 [28, 33] cm)

ADD YOUR EMBELLISHMENTS!

With CC, cast on 2 sts and knit 2 i-cord strands, each measuring approximately 14" (35.5 cm) long. Weave I-cord through the top edge of mukluk, right under the rib portion, at about 1" (2.5 cm) intervals. The cords should meet at the outer edges of each slipper so that you can tie them into a bow or loose knot. Use the photo for reference.

Using Wildflower Yarn, make 2 tassels, approximately 2" (5 cm) long, to add to the I-cord tie edges. Using the Clover mini pom-pom maker, make 2 pom-poms approximately 1" (2.5 cm) in diameter. (The sample used both the remaining MC and CC in the pom-poms.) Attach the pom-poms and tassels wherever you like along the i-cord edge. (The sample has one of each on the bottom of each tie, so each mukluk has one pom-pom on the bottom edge and one tassel.) Sew your pom-pom and tassels to the i-cord edges with a needle and thread and you're all set to wear your slippers with a smile!

SILTUMS SCARF

suzanne middlebrooks

6" (15 cm)

60" (152.5 cm)

SUZANNE MIDDLEBROOKS

is the owner of Hill Country Weavers in Austin, Texas. Her shop carries the largest selection of yarn and knitting, crochet, weaving, and felting tools in the area and offers classes and events to support all aspects of the fiber arts community. Get a glimpse at her gorgeous shop through the tour in Episode 110 of *The Knit Show.*

MATERIALS
3 hanks Naturally HCW Hippie Hollow (50% Highland wool, 50% superfine alpaca; 54 yd/100 g): Grey

Size U.S. 19 (15 mm) needles —*or size needed to obtain gauge*

Tapestry needle

FINISHED MEASUREMENTS
5" (12.75 cm) wide, 60" (152.5 cm) long, excluding pom-poms

GAUGE
10 sts x 8 rows = 4" (10 cm) in Rick Rack Stitch, unstretched

DIRECTIONS

Using the cable cast-on method, CO 13 stitches.

Row 1: *P1, knit into the back loop of the second stitch on your left needle, knit into the front loop of the first stitch on your left needle, slide both stitches off the left needle. Repeat from * to last stitch, p1.

Row 2: *K1, purl into the second stitch on your left needle, purl into the first stitch on your left needle, slide both stitches off the left needle. Repeat from * to last stitch, k1.

Rick Rack Stitch established.

Repeat Rows 1 and 2 until piece measures 60" (152.5 cm).

BO all stitches loosely.

FINISHING
Using desired method, make two pom-poms approx. 3" (7.5 cm) in diameter. Sew pom-poms to ends of scarf, gathering all the stitches at each end to form a point. Weave in ends. Block, if necessary.

THE
KNOWLEDGE

THE BEGINNINGS

E-Wrap Cast-On
Cable Cast-On
German Twisted (aka old
  Norwegian) Cast-On
Indian Cast-On
Judy's Magic Cast-On

THE MIDDLES

Magic Loop
Chain Plying
Portuguese Purl
Russian Join

THE ENDINGS

Wendy's SSK Bind-Off
Jeny's Surprisingly
  Stretchy Bind-Off
Kitchener Stitch
  (Stockinette)
Russian Grafting
Swiss Darning

THE BEGINNINGS

E-WRAP CAST-ON

This cast-on is perfect for adding stitches at the end or middle of a row!

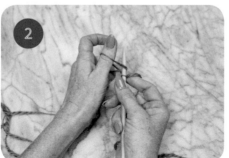

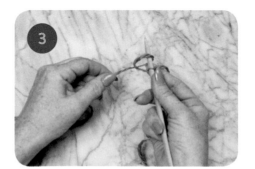

1. Wrap the working yarn around your thumb clockwise, letting it hang. You'll see a backward loop around your thumb that resembles a cursive, lowercase "e."

2. With a knitting needle in your right hand, bring the needle up through the loop on your thumb.

3. Remove your thumb while simultaneously pulling the working yarn so the stitch is secured (but not too tight) on the needle.

Repeat until desired amount of stitches are cast on.

CABLE CAST-ON

This method gives a more elastic edge than the Single or Long Tail method. It's particularly great for casting on extra stitches in the middle of a project.

This cast-on requires that you already have at least two stitches on your needle to begin with.

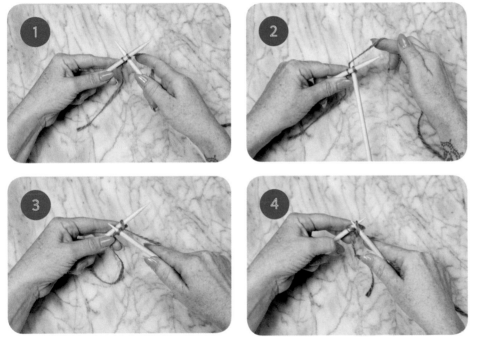

1. Insert the right-hand needle into the space between the last two stitches.

2. Wrap yarn counterclockwise around the right-hand needle.

3. Pull the loop through the space.

4. Slip the new stitch onto the left-hand needle.

   Repeat until you have cast on the desired number of stitches.

GERMAN TWISTED (AKA OLD NORWEGIAN) CAST-ON

This cast-on is the stretchier sister to the Long Tail method. It's great for Brioche Stitch projects, necklines, and cuffs!

1. Choose a length of yarn for tail (will vary based on amount of stitches needed).

   Letting the tail hang, tie a slipknot around a knitting needle. You'll now have two strands of yarn.

2. Take the needle in your right hand, and with your thumb and pointer finger on your left hand, separate the two strands of yarn.

3. Secure both loose ends under your ring finger and pinky (if you pull the needle down toward your palm, you'll see that loops have formed around both fingers and will look vaguely like a slingshot).

4. Take the needle and swoop under both strands of yarn on your thumb.

5. Dip the needle down through the loop on the thumb (5A), then sweep up to grab the strand of yarn around your pointer finger (5B), bringing the strand down and through the opening under where the thumb-yarn crosses (5C).

6. Let go; tighten.

   Repeat process until desired number of stitches are cast on.

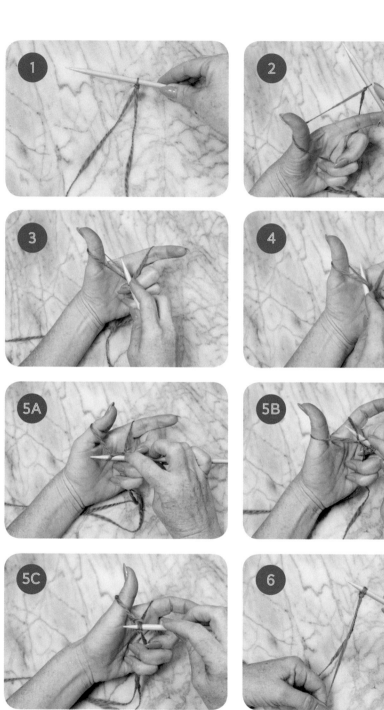

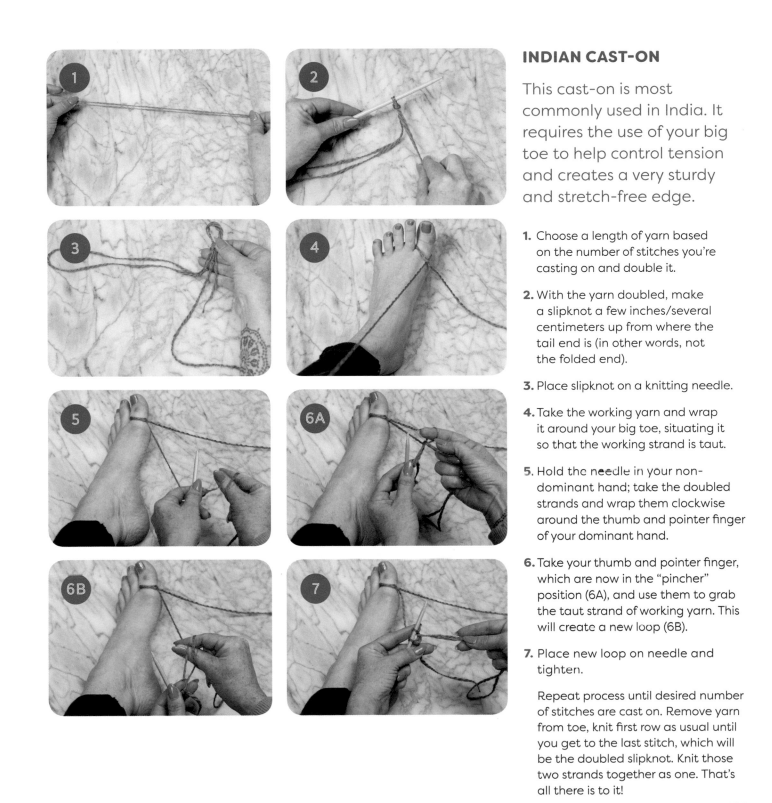

INDIAN CAST-ON

This cast-on is most commonly used in India. It requires the use of your big toe to help control tension and creates a very sturdy and stretch-free edge.

1. Choose a length of yarn based on the number of stitches you're casting on and double it.

2. With the yarn doubled, make a slipknot a few inches/several centimeters up from where the tail end is (in other words, not the folded end).

3. Place slipknot on a knitting needle.

4. Take the working yarn and wrap it around your big toe, situating it so that the working strand is taut.

5. Hold the needle in your non-dominant hand; take the doubled strands and wrap them clockwise around the thumb and pointer finger of your dominant hand.

6. Take your thumb and pointer finger, which are now in the "pincher" position (6A), and use them to grab the taut strand of working yarn. This will create a new loop (6B).

7. Place new loop on needle and tighten.

Repeat process until desired number of stitches are cast on. Remove yarn from toe, knit first row as usual until you get to the last stitch, which will be the doubled slipknot. Knit those two strands together as one. That's all there is to it!

JUDY'S MAGIC CAST-ON

This cast-on, invented by Judy Becker, really does work like magic, as it casts on two rows of stitches at the same time! This method is intended for working socks from the toe up.

1. With a length of yarn based on the number of desired stitches, place a slipknot on one dpn or one of the needles of a circular (if you're knitting using the Magic Loop method).

2. Grab a second dpn, or the second needle of the circular, and hold it parallel with the needle with the slipknot in back.

3. Like with the commonly used Long Tail or German cast-ons, there will be two strands of yarn hanging, which you will hold in the same manner as for those methods.

   Swoop the front needle up and under the farthest (from you) strand of yarn on your pointer finger (3A), scooping the strand of yarn off of your finger and onto the needle (this will create a version of the E-Wrap, opposite, cast on to that front needle); pull taut (3B).

4. Then take the back needle and swoop up and under the closest (to you) strand of yarn on your thumb, scooping the strand off of your thumb and onto the needle, creating a stitch on the back needle.

   Repeat process until desired number of stitches have been cast on.

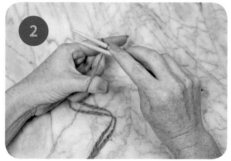

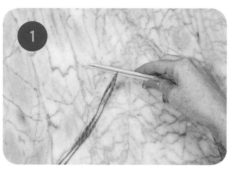

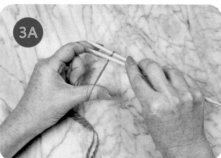

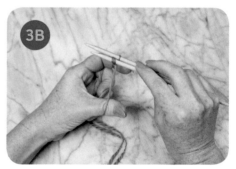

THE MIDDLES

CHAIN PLYING

Chain plying (sometimes known as Navajo knitting) uses a spinning technique to triple-ply yarn to make a thicker fiber. This is a great option for tuning a fingering weight into a more practical, heavier weight, but is also really fun when applied to already bulky yarns.

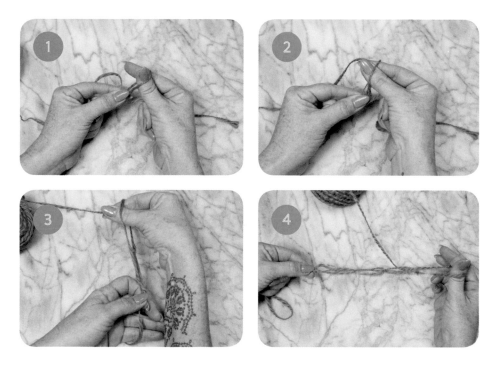

1. Make a slipknot; slide your dominant hand's fingers through the loop of the slipknot (holding the knot firmly with opposite hand).

2. Grab the working yarn and pull the strand through the loop. You'll see three strands formed. The length of these strands is totally your preference, but this overall effect is what you want.

3. Continue grabbing the working yarn strand and pulling it through to create new, long loops, until you have at least enough to cast on for your project with.

4. Once you begin knitting, treating your newly plied yarn as if it were single-plied, you can create more lengths of plies as you go.

MAGIC LOOP

The Magic Loop earns its name because it negates the need for a specific length circular needle, or multiple double-pointed needles. Using this method, you can knit any circumference using one long circular needle.

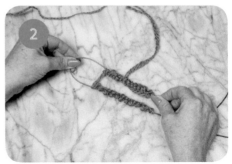

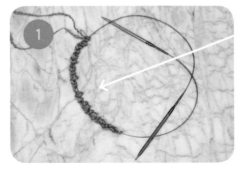

1. Cast on number of stitches required by pattern.

   Move the stitches to the center point of cable and find the middle of the stitches (as even as possible).

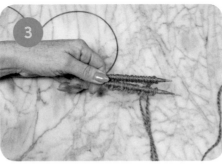

2. Pull the cable through the center point of the stitches, creating a loop.

3. Push stitches so that half are sitting on the front needle and half on the back needle.

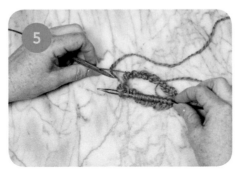

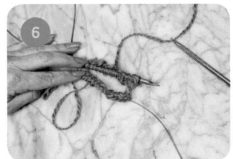

4. Pull the back needle out so that the back half of the stitches are resting on the cable, making the back needle usable.

   Join round by knitting the first stitch on the front needle.

5. Knit all stitches on the front needle; readjust cord so that back stitches are now on a needle, and front needle is usable to knit with.

6. Knit the rest of the round.

7. Continue in this manner for all rounds.

PORTUGUESE PURL

My friend Patty Lyons taught me this method as a fix for the inconsistency in purl stitch gauge that can be the result of a looser grasp on yarn when purling, versus knitting. Much like the Indian use of a big toe to control tension for their cast-on (see page 191), the Portuguese use their necks as guides for yarn.

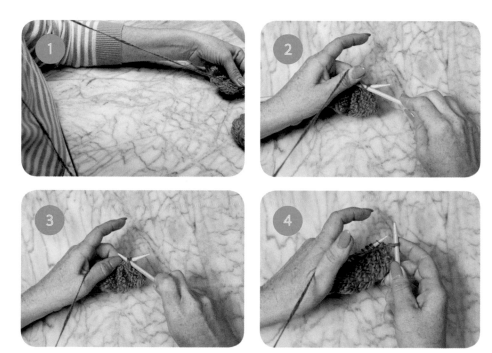

1. Wrap the working yarn, from left to right, around the back of your neck, letting the ball sit on your right side.

2. Insert needle purlwise into stitch.

3. Use your left thumb to "flick" (wrap) the yarn around the needle.

4. Push the right needle through to create the new stitch, letting the old stitch drop off of the needle.

RUSSIAN JOIN

This is a method for joining two strands of yarn when you don't have a long enough tail to weave in later and the yarn will not felt together. It works best with plied yarn.

1. Lay end of new strand of yarn over old one.

2. Thread end of one strand of yarn through tapestry needle, leaving about a 1" (2.5 cm) tail.

   Turn the needle back and bury into the plies of the working yarn, drawing through about 2" (5 cm).

   Pull the needle and short tail. Remove needle.

   Thread the second (new) strand of yarn through the tapestry needle; turn the needle back and bury into the plies of the working yarn, drawing through about 2" (5 cm).

3. Tug the yarn ends so that join is complete.

4. Trim ends.

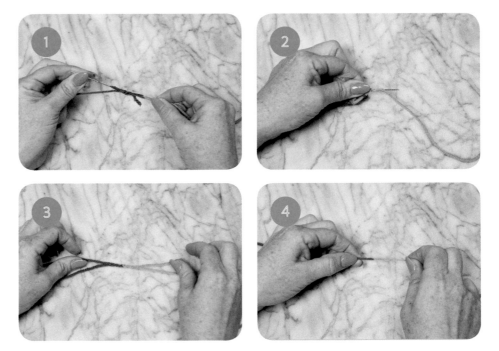

THE ENDINGS

WENDY'S SSK BIND-OFF

This bind-off was taught to me (and we think invented) by Wendy Moreland. The intention behind this method is to create a more even edge than obtained by the pulling of stitches as they're passed over, as in the traditional bind-off.

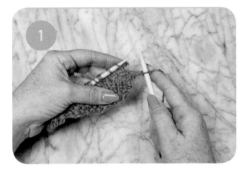

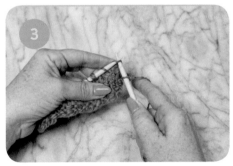

1. Knit the first stitch on the left-hand needle.

2. *Slip the next stitch knitwise.

3. Knit both stitches on the right-hand needle together, through the back loop.

   Repeat from * until all stitches are bound off.

KITCHENER STITCH

This technique seamlessly joins two Stockinette Stitch pieces of fabric together.

1. Set up:

Place an equal number of stitches on two needles and hold parallel.

2. Insert tapestry needle **purlwise** into the first stitch on FRONT needle.

3. Pull tail through, but don't let the stitch fall off.

4. Insert tapestry needle **knitwise** into the first stitch on the BACK needle.

5. Pull tail through, but don't let the stitch fall off.

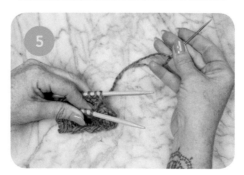

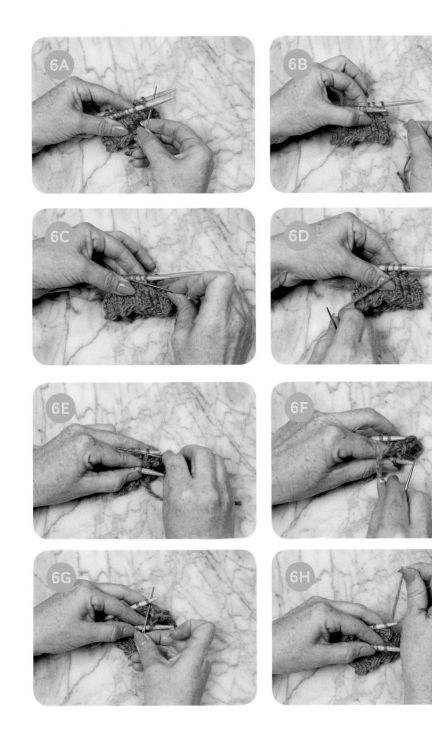

6. Begin grafting:

*Insert tapestry needle **knitwise** into the first stitch on the FRONT needle (6A) and pull tail through, letting it fall off the knitting needle (6B).

Insert tapestry needle **purlwise** into the next stitch on the FRONT needle (6C) and pull the tail through, WITHOUT letting the stitch fall off the knitting needle (6D).

Insert tapestry needle **purlwise** into the first stitch on the BACK needle (6E) and pull tail through, letting it fall off the knitting needle (6F).

Insert tapestry needle **knitwise** into the next stitch on the FRONT needle (6G) and pull the tail through, WITHOUT letting the stitch fall off the knitting needle (6H).

Repeat from * until all stitches are grafted.

JENY'S SURPRISINGLY STRETCHY BIND-OFF

This ribbed bind-off was invented by Jeny Saimen (aka Curious Knitter) as the jelly to the peanut butter of Judy's Magic Cast-On (see page 192) for knitting socks from the toe up.

It gives you more fabric, thereby allowing for a nice, stretchy finish!

1. Setting up for a knit stitch, begin with a yarn-over **backward** (so, from back to front); (1A) knit the stitch (1B).

2. Pass the yarn-over over the knit stitch on the right-hand needle, letting it drop off.

3. Setting up for a purl stitch, yarn-over as normal (so, from front to back); purl the stitch.

   At the same time, pass BOTH the yarn-over and the second stitch on the right-hand needle over the purl stitch, letting it drop off.

4. Yarn-over **backward**. Knit 1.

5. Pass both the yarn-over and the second stitch on the right-hand needle over the stitch, letting it drop off.

6. Continue in this manner until all stitches are bound off.

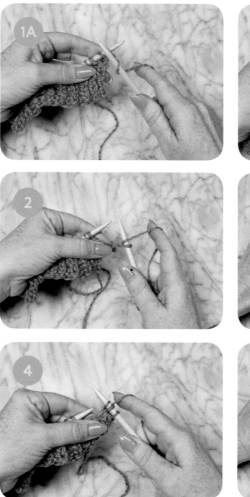

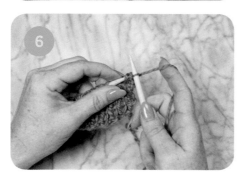

SWISS DARNING

Swiss Darning, aka Duplicate Stitch, is a method both for reinforcing worn Stockinette Stitches and for adding contrasting stitches to duplicate those below for small pictures (in lieu of using the intarsia method), or for personalizing with initials.

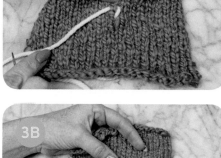

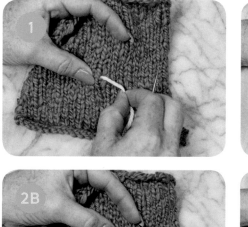

1. Using tapestry needle and yarn, come up through the base (the bottom of the "V") of a knit stitch.

2. Insert needle under both loops of the stitch above the one you're duplicating (2A–2B).

3. Pull the yarn through and go back down through the point of the "V" where you started (3A–3B).

RUSSIAN GRAFTING

Instead of a tapestry needle, this method uses a crochet hook. Unlike Kitchener Stitch, Russian Grafting is not meant to be seamless. Instead, it offers a join with a decorative flair!

1. Set up:

   Place an equal number of stitches on two needles and hold parallel.

2. Insert crochet hook **knitwise** into stitch on BACK needle and pull stitch off onto hook.

3. Insert crochet hook **knitwise** into stitch on FRONT needle (3A) and pull stitch off onto hook and through the first stitch on hook (3B).

4. Continue grafting:

   *Insert crochet hook **knitwise** into stitch on BACK needle (4A) and pull stitch off of the needle and through the stitch on hook (4B).

5. Insert crochet hook **knitwise** into stitch on FRONT needle (5A) and pull stitch off the needle and through the stitch on hook (5B).

6. Repeat from * until all stitches are grafted.

alt = alternate

approx = approximately

beg = begin/beginning

bet = between

BO = bind off

BP = back post

bpdc = back post double crochet

bpdc2tog = back post double crochet 2 together

BPdtr = back post double treble crochet

BPhdc = back post half double crochet

BPsc = back post single crochet

BPtr = back post triple crochet

byo = backward yarn-over

CC = contrasting color

ch = chain

ch-sp = chain space

cont = continue

dc = double crochet

dec = decrease

dc2tog = double crochet 2 together

edc = extended double crochet

ehdc = extended half double crochet

esc = extended single crochet

etr = extended treble crochet

FL or FLO = front loop or front loop only

foll = following

FP = front post

fpdc = front post double crochet

FPhdc = front post half double crochet

FPsc = front post single crochet

FPtr = front post treble crochet

hdc = half double crochet

hdc2tog = half double crochet 2 stitches together

inc = increase

k = knit

k1B = knit stitch in row below

kfb = knit 1 into front and back of stitch

ksp = knit 1 stitch, slip this stitch from right needle to left needle, pass second stitch on left needle over first stitch and off left needle; return stitch to right needle; single right-leaning decrease

k2tog = knit 2 stitches together; single right-leaning decrease

kwise = knitwise

lp = loop

m = marker

M1 = make 1 stitch

M1L - make 1 left slanting

M1R = make 1 right slanting

M1p = make 1 purlwise

M1lp = make 1 left slanting, purlwise

M1lr = make 1 right slanting, purlwise

MC = main color

p = purl

patt = pattern

pfb = purl into front and back of stitch

pm = place marker

p2tog = purl 2 stitches together

prev = previous

psso = pass slipped stitches

PU = pick up

pwise = purlwise

rem = remaining

rep = repeat

rev St st = reverse Stockinette stitch

RH = right hand

RS = Right Side

rnd = round

sc = single crochet

sc2tog = single crochet 2 together

sk = skip

SKP = slip 1 knitwise, knit 1, pass slip stitch over knit stitch

SK2P = slip 1 knitwise, knit 2 together, pass slip stitch over knit-together stitches

sl = slip

sl1k = slip 1 knitwise

sl1p = slip 1 purlwise

sl m = slip marker

sl st = slip stitch

sp = space

ssk = slip 2 stitches knitwise, knit these 2 stitches together through the back loops

ssp = slip 2 sts knitwise, return these 2 stitches to left needle and purl them together through the back loops

sssk = slip 3 stitches knitwise, knit these 3 stitches together through the back loops

sssp = slip 3 sts knitwise, return these 3 stitches to left needle and purl them together through the back loops

st(s) = stitch(es)

tbl = through back loop

tch or t-ch = turning chain

tfl = through the front loop

tog = together

tr = triple crochet

tr2tog = triple crochet 2 stitches together

WS = wrong side

w & t = wrap and turn

wyib = with yarn in back

wyif = with yarn in front

yb = yarn back

yf = yarn forward

yo = yarn-over

U.S. TO U.K. CROCHET TERM CONVERSIONS

single crochet (sc) = double crochet (dc)

double crochet (dc) = treble crochet (tr)

half double crochet (hdc) = half treble crochet (htr)

triple crochet (tr) = double treble (dtr)

Allred Leather Company
allredleathercompany.com

Andrea Brinkley
oandystudio.com

B.hooked
bhookedcrochet.com

Blue Sky Fibers
blueskyfibers.com

Boyland Knitworks
boylandknitworks.com

Brini Maxwell
brinimaxwell.com

Bristol Ivy
bristolivy.com

Chelsea DeKryuff, MA, LPC
chelseadekruyff.com

Clinton Hill Cashmere
clintonhillcashmere.com

Christiane Knight
xiane.org

Drew Emborsky
thecrochetdude.com

Energy Muse
energymuse.com

Erika Knight
erikaknight.co.uk

Ewe Ewe Yarns
eweewe.com

The Farmer's Daughter Fibers
thefarmersdaughterfibers.com

Independence Wool
independencewool.com

Hill Country Weavers
hillcountryweavers.com

Jeny Staiman
ravelry.com/designers/jeny-staiman

Josh Bennett
joshbennettnyc.com

Judy Becker
ravelry.com/designers/judy-becker

Judy Hall Crystals
judyhall.co.uk

Julia Madill
ravelry.com/designers/julia-madill

Kelbourne Woolens
kelbournewoolens.com

Knit Collage
knitcollage.com

Koigu
koigu.com

Kristin Omdahl Yarns
kristinomdahl.com

La Bien Aimee
labienaimee.com

London Kaye
londonkaye.com

Malabrigo Yarns
malabrigoyarn.com

Nancy Marchant
briochestitch.com

Nicky Epstein
nickyepstein.com

Marly Bird
marlybird.com

Plump & Co (NZ)
plumpandco.com

The Practical Numerologist
feliciabender.com

Red Heart Yarn
redheart.com/chicsheep

Siedah Garrett
siedah.com

Valley Yarns
yarn.com

Vogue Knitting magazine
vogueknitting.com

Welcome Blanket
welcomeblanket.org

Yarn Standards
yarnstandards.com

Yarnspirations
yarnspirations.com

Zauberball Cotton
skacelknitting.com

The outfit Kaffe Fassett designed with Bill Gibb (discussed on pages 15–16) can be found here: www.fashionmuseum.co.uk/sites/fashion_museum/files/styles/portrait_thumbnail/public/1970.jpg

VICKIE HOWELL is an award-winning broadcast personality, producer, author, designer, speaker, and instructor in the D.I.Y. world and beyond. Her 2018 People's Telly Award–winning and Webby Award–honoree groundbreaking series *The Knit Show with Vickie Howell* (YouTube) is the first studio-funded, community-funded, internationally accessible knitting and crochet streaming series. As of the writing of this book, there have been over 350,000 views by people in at least twenty countries.

Vickie is also well-known as the host of TV shows such as DIY Network's *Knitty Gritty* and *Stylelicious* and PBS's *Knitting Daily with Vickie Howell*; for her bestselling knitting, crochet, and craft books; and for her accessible, inclusive approach to nurturing the creative community via print, video, and social media.

Vickie's designs and projects have been included in hundreds of publications world-wide; she's been the ambassador for major brands in the United States, Canada, and the United Kingdom and continues her passion for motivating and inspiring people to both live creatively *and* make a living being creative. Her Facebook Live series (the first and longest-running of its kind in the genre), *Ask Me Monday*; online courses for *CreativeLive* and *Brit+Co.*; her podcast, *Craft*ish*; and her popular subscription-box business, YarnYAY!, are all elements of the total voice Vickie uses to preach the importance of breathing in, crafting out.

Follow all of Vickie's projects on social media. You can find her @vickiehowell everywhere except Pinterest, where she's @iamvickiehowell.

acknowledgment

Big ups to my editor, Shawna Mullen, for the conversations over a year to decide what type of book we'd like to make together, then giving me the room to let it happen on my own time.

Thank you so much to Onethread Design and Deb Wood for making this book look as beautiful as I'd envisioned and to Kathleen Gaffney for wrangling the massive amount of elements within it.

Big, mushy-gushy appreciation to my sister from another mister, Traci Goudie, for taking time from your director/producer gigs to take the photos for this book. It means the world to me that we shared this project!

Thank you to my family, who have borne yet another book-writing experience with me. To Clover, for making sure I always had sparkling water and ginger chews during long writing sessions; to Tristan, my new, literally in-house schematic illustrator, for making that whole process so much easier; to Tanner, for your words of encouragement and the promise to come home from college to visit me in the asylum should this be the book that finally pushes me over the edge; and to my rock, Dave, for making sure the household ran, so I could soar while working on this project. You are my everything.

Thank you so much to sisters-in-law Alicia Montoya and Meredith Smith, who, respectively, lent their time (and faces) to travel to Austin to model for this book. It was important to me to have representation of beautiful but different women in their forties included. I feel extremely grateful that they're also women whom I love.

Thanks also to my mother-in-law, Debi Campbell, who stepped in to assist whenever we needed a second set of family logistics hands. You were a huge help!

I am so fortunate to have a wonderful support group of friends, ready to listen or make me laugh when I need it most. Sending so much love and appreciation to every one of you.